Seven Tips to Make the Most
of the
Camino de Santiago

Seven Tips to Make the Most of the Camino de Santiago

By

Cheri Powell

R. C. Linnell Publishing

Seven Tips to Make the Most of the Camino de Santiago

Cover design by Dave Davis.

ISBN-10: 0615381464

ISBN-13: 978-0-615-38146-6

Short Stories by Cheri Powell:

A Case of Need
Proximity
Necessary Data

Check out her website at:

www.CheriPowell.com

email: Camino_Cheri@yahoo.com

For Rick

May we always walk the path together.

Acknowledgments

Nothing is ever done in a vacuum. Many friends have graciously given their time toward this project. Special thanks goes to Sheri Orbesen who has read every word of this book several times over. Gail Lobred and Laurie Huff have read all or parts of the manuscript and given feedback.

Peggy DeKay and the Women Who Write group opened my eyes to the possibility of self-publishing and gave the direction that got me started.

Hopscotch House retreats gave me time away from distractions to write, edit and review this manuscript.

Dave and Kristin Davis gave invaluable help with the cover and associated web page.

The most gratitude goes to my husband Rick, who shared the journey and became my helpmate in getting this written and published. I could not have done it without you.

To everyone who contributed: Thank you one and all.

Table of Contents

Introduction

The decision to walk the Camino was easy. The preparation was the hard part. It took five years of research, education, and planning before we finally boarded the plane for Spain. Even with all the groundwork, there were surprises. After talking to other pilgrims along the way, we discovered that some of the "surprises" were universal. Those conversations sparked the stimulus for this book.

Not everyone is interested in a spiritual pilgrimage and many in the United States think of pilgrimages as something done only in the past. Awareness of the sites and the close proximity lets more Europeans participate in pilgrimages. Spain's 2010 World Cup soccer win catapulted the Camino de Santiago to American newspapers when it was announced that the coach had vowed the whole team would walk the Camino if they won the cup. Many Spanish soccer fans plan to do likewise.

This book is intended to help the prospective pilgrim get organized before boarding the plane. The seven tips presented provide a foundation for the preparation. Further reading will round that out.

Travel technology is constantly updated and this affects the items taken and how the trip may be accomplished. Any useful, emerging technology is presented in the lists of items.

You will leave this book at home after reading it. It will probably be dog-eared and have notes written in the margins. That is its intended use. I purposely chose a large book size with side margins. Get out your pencils and scribble on the page. Highlight as necessary. There are extra pages in the back for additional notes. This is your workbook for getting to the Camino.

I had originally planned to include pictures to illustrate parts of the book. However, the printing costs would have increased the selling price four fold. To keep costs and the price reasonable, no pictures are included in the book, but they are on my website – www.CheriPowell.com. I have also included a downloadable version of the cost calculation spreadsheet in Appendix C. Visit often.

You will never regret your decision to undertake a spiritual pilgrimage. You will see yourself and the world from a different perspective for the rest of your life. I am glad I could play a small part to propel you on your journey.

Buen Camino!

Cheri Powell
www.CheriPowell.com
Camino_Cheri@yahoo.com

Tip #1

Know the History of the Camino

People tend to forget that the word "history" contains the word "story."
Ken Burns

If you would know the road ahead, ask someone who has traveled it.
Chinese Proverb

The more one knows about the background of something, the more interesting the thing itself is. For an undertaking like the Camino, the history is essential for understanding what you will see along the way.

Tip #1 – Know the History of the Camino

Who was St. James?

Before any pilgrimages along the Camino there was St. James. Before there was St. James, there was James, Son of Zebedee who worked as a fisherman in Jerusalem. James and his brother John left their jobs and family to follow Jesus. They, along with Peter, became intimate friends of Jesus and are present at many important times in Jesus' life, such as being present in the garden of Gethsemane before the crucifixion and when Jesus cured Peter's mother-in-law. James is mentioned a few times in the books of Matthew, Mark, Luke and Acts. He is known as Saint James the Greater to distinguish him from the other apostle who was younger and known as Saint James the Less.

Both James and John were boisterous young men and sometimes had unchecked tempers. Because of this they both gained the nickname "Boanerges" which means "Sons of Thunder." On one occasion they wanted Jesus to destroy a Samaritan town with a rain of fire when the inhabitants did not welcome Him. They raised the ire of the other apostles, when they requested to be on the right and left hand of Jesus in His kingdom. Jesus chastised them on these and other occasions, teaching them a bit of humility and patience.

After the crucifixion, the apostles went to different parts of the world to spread the Gospel. James went to the Iberian Peninsula (what is now Spain) and spent several years trying to convert the local people. His effectiveness and success is debated, as a few accounts say he only had seven followers when, in the year 44, he decided to go back to Jerusalem. Herod Agrippa, who was still in power in Jerusalem, engaged in political battles by persecuting Christians to please the Jews. Consequently, because of James' close association with Jesus, Herod had James beheaded. Thus, James became the first apostolic martyr and the second Christian martyr, after Stephen. It is at this point that documented history and legend start to intertwine.

James' followers gathered up his beheaded remains with the intention of taking them back to the Iberian Peninsula. Legends say they crossed the Mediterranean in a stone boat with no sails or rudder. The boat navigated the sea easily and landed on what is now the Galacian coast of Spain. The miraculous voyage is reputed to have taken only a week. An actual voyage would have taken several weeks. James' followers took his decapitated body and his head inland near the city of Iria Flavia (now El Padron) to bury them.   Local custom dictated that permission for burial had to be obtained from the current ruler, Queen Lupa. As was usual with such a request, the queen presented a test to the followers to prove their worthiness. She sent out two fierce bulls to guard the site and keep them away. However, James' followers were able to tame the bulls and thus gain the right to perform the burial. Two of James' followers, Theodore and Athanasius maintained the shrine until their deaths and then were buried next to him.

The site was forgotten for about 800 years. Many political and economic changes took place during this time including an invasion by the Moors. These were troubling times for both Christians and Muslims, as there were constant battles and skirmishes for control and power in the small kingdoms that made up what we now call Spain. Around the year 833, Islam was the prevalent religion and Muslims were the conquering army. Then things began to change. New lights appeared in the sky and shone down on a particular spot near the Galacian coast. Pelayo, a religious hermit, followed the lights and re-discovered Saint James' bones. A local bishop identified the bones as belonging to Saint James. They were reburied and a small church was built on the site.

The timing of the discovery was fortuitous, as the Christian warriors were disheartened and losing their fight against the Moors who had

Mohammed's arm bone as a talisman to encourage them in battle. At this time the spirit of Saint James appeared on a white stallion brandishing a sword and gave the Christians new vigor to drive out the Moors. Thus, Saint James now became Saint James the Moorslayer (Santiago Matamoros). He appeared several times between the years 1100 and 1200 in this guise and gained fame for his Moor slaying encouragement. Five of the twenty-two miracles attributed to him involve soldiers and combat.

The city where the small church was built with the newly discovered remains of Saint James came to be called Compostela. There is some debate about the origin of the name. Some historians think it is a form of "campo de las estrellas" or field of stars. Others think it may be derived from Latin words meaning "pretty place" or "burial land." Whatever the provenience, the city quickly grew in size and became famous. The Christian effort to re-conquer the area was greatly aided by its connection to the apostle and by all the various religious and secular officials who would benefit from a Christian victory. By the year 883, a larger church had been built over the saint's remains.

As word spread about the miracles of Santiago and the location of his remains, the number of pilgrims to the site increased. This caused homes to be turned into rooming houses and restaurants along the way. Candle makers were needed for the increased demand for candles by the pilgrims. Pilgrims wanted to take home a memento of their journey, and so craftsmen began making items that could be easily carried home. Associated businesses began to spring up and The Camino de Santiago (Way of St. James) became an industry.

First Pilgrim's Guide

The popularity of The Camino has waxed and waned throughout the years. During the twelfth century, in about the year 1140, a remarkable document was written by a pilgrim. It is known as the

Liber Sancti Jacobi and contains five books about Saint James, his miracles and a pilgrimage to Santiago. Four copies survive, and one copy, known as the Codex Calixtinus, is housed at the library of the Cathedral in Santiago. Translations of the work are in print today and offer insight, not only into the history of St James, but into the daily life and political issues of the twelfth century.

The first and longest book in the Liber Sancti contains liturgical material and music for the feast day (July 25) of Santiago. The second book gives details of the twenty-two miracles attributed to Saint James. The third book tells the story of his martyrdom and how his remains came to be located in Compostela. The fourth book is reputed to have been written by Turpin, Charlemagne's Archbishop of Reins and contains the tales of the battles of Charlemagne and Roland against the Moors.

The fifth book is a pilgrim's guide to the Camino. It tells the prospective pilgrim about the route to take and what is available along the way in terms of places to eat and where to stay. It is probably one of the oldest tourist guides still in existence and provided information for countless pilgrims during the latter part of the Middle Ages. The pilgrimage was quite popular until about the eighteenth century, when fewer people took an interest in making the journey. That changed on January 28, 1879 when an excavation found three skeletons buried beneath the Santiago Cathedral. These remains were proclaimed to be those of Santiago and his two followers, Theodore and Athanasius. The claim was supported in 1884 by a Papal Bull by Pope Leo XIII which stated that they were authentic. Santiago's remains were re-interred in a silver casket which can now be viewed in the Santiago Cathedral.

Miracles of St. James

The miracles of Saint James offer some insight into the popularity of the pilgrimage. Of the twenty-two miracles, four are releases from prison or slavery, two provide forgiveness, six are healings, nine describe people being saved from some calamity and one involves opening gates at the cathedral. Saint James does not necessarily appear or speak in all of the miracles, but through other evidence, they are all attributed to him. They all take place between 800 and 1200, with the majority being in the 1100's. The nationality of the recipients, when known, is European, with most of them French. All but three of the recipients were pilgrims, and had their miracles occur, either before a pilgrimage, which inspired them to go, during a pilgrimage, or as a result of a pilgrimage. All but six of the miracles occurred along what is today known as the French route to Santiago.

The content of these miracles makes interesting reading, but by far the most interesting and most repeated miracle involves a young man and his parents, who were making the pilgrimage together in the year 1090. It is miracle number five and many variations have sprung up in legends, stories, and plays. The gist of the story is that the family stopped for lodging one night along the road. One version involves an evil innkeeper putting silver in the knapsack of either the father or the son. In the morning, the "theft" is discovered and the father and son are accused. They are taken before the local judge who takes pity on them and decrees that only one should be punished and the one freed. The punishment is rather severe: hanging. Both father and son want to sacrifice themselves for the other, but in the end, the father is set free and the son is hanged. The father continues the pilgrimage to Compostela and pays homage to St. James at the altar in the cathedral. On the return trip, the father again goes to the same town to visit his son's body, which was still hanging. Upon seeing the body, he begins to cry in anguish and to his astonishment, the son answers him, telling him that Saint James revived him and continues to hold his body aloft so that the hangman's noose does no damage. The father rejoices and brings the townspeople to witness the miracle. They realize their error and promptly hang the innkeeper. The moral of the story is to urge

Christians to be diligent in investigating crimes of this sort, because they may be duped by fraudulent people.

Another, more common version has the family staying at a house in the city of Santo Domingo de la Calzada, where the daughter of the owner is attracted to the son. When he spurns her advances, she takes silver from her house and puts it in his knapsack. In the morning, she accuses him of theft and he is promptly arrested, tried and hanged. The parents continue to Compostela, where the mother hears her son's voice saying he is still alive thanks to the intervention of Saint James and the Virgin Mary. They return to the town of Santo Domingo de la Calzada and go to see the judge who sentenced their son. He is eating and does not believe the parent's story. He tells the parents that their son is "as alive as the roasted hen and rooster" on his dining table. At that moment, the hen and the rooster, regained their feathers, came back to life, and flew off the table. The astonished judge took the parents to where the boy was and discovered that he was indeed alive. The regenerated rooster and hen were taken to the local church as proof of the miracle. Today, in the church in the city of Santo Domingo de la Calzada, one can see a live rooster and a hen kept in a comfortable cage as proof of the miracle. The honor is given to a new pair each week, and the replaced pair feed the poor. To this day, it is considered good luck to find a chicken feather or to hear a rooster crow along the Camino.

Modern Camino

When one compares the few times that James is mentioned in the Bible with the amount of literature subsequently written about him, a rather large discrepancy occurs. What made this particular saint accumulate such fame? Aside from the desire of the Christians for a guiding spirit during the wars against the Moors, part of the reason can be attributed to strong supporters, who embellished the miracles in stories which subsequently became legends. During the Middle Ages, there was a movement to remove Saint James as the patron saint of Spain and replace him with Saint Teresa of Avila. Saint James' supporters turned out to be better organized and they responded by writing letters to the Vatican, and retelling the miracles in the form of stories and legends so that Saint James became the favorite choice of the people. His reign as Patron Saint has since been uncontested.

Political and economic issues have also played a part. Pilgrims along the way need a place to sleep and something to eat. In early times, the churches provided shelter and food, but space was limited. Farmers, who had houses or barns, would let pilgrims stay in them. As the number of pilgrims increased establishments were built just for the pilgrims and the economy of the towns along the way became dependent on the pilgrim trade. Officials supported this, as it brought added prosperity to the area.

The popularity and fame of Santiago went with the explorers to the New World. There is a city named Santiago in Chile, Guatemala, Argentina, Cuba and the Dominican Republic. There is a Matamoros, Mexico. There is a Fort Santiago in Manila in the Philippines. Also most cities of any size in Central or South America have at least one street named Santiago or Matamoros. Various locations, parks and buildings also carry the name. It is also a common name given to male babies in Spanish speaking areas.

The last twenty years have seen a dramatic increase in the number of pilgrims. In 1985, a mere 2,491 pilgrims made the trek. In 1993, a Holy Year for Saint James, there were 99,436 pilgrims. The number decreases in non Holy Years, but still has been steadily increasing overall. The last Holy Year, 2004, saw 179,944 pilgrims qualify for the Compostela. In 2005, the year we went, there were 93,924 pilgrims of which 3,991 were from North America. In 2008, there were a total of 125,141 pilgrims from 108 countries. The number of pilgrims from the USA ranks sixth with 2,214 pilgrims. The European countries had the most pilgrims with their numbers being Spain 61,112; Germany 15,746; Italy 10,707; France 6.618 and Portugal 4,341.

Numbers this large have obviously had an impact on the local economies. Holy Years (when the saint's feast day falls on a Sunday) offer a time when extra effort goes into updating the amenities along the Camino. The Catholic Church made a special effort to accommodate pilgrims for the 2004 Holy Year and many new albergues were built or existing ones expanded and updated in anticipation of the large number of expected pilgrims. The same effort was undertaken in anticipation of the 2010 Holy Year. Today it is easier and more enjoyable on many levels to make this pilgrimage.

Today, the pilgrim holds a special status. They are easily identified by their backpack, cockle shell, and staff as they walk through city and countryside. Natives along the way will smile, wave and shout "Buen Camino!" or "Ultreya" as pilgrims pass by. The pilgrim represents not only a spiritual seeker and someone to be respected, but someone who helps the local economy and keeps the tradition of Camino de Santiago alive and strong.

Tip #1 Takeaways

- ❖ Saint James, the first apostolic martyr, preached on the Iberian Peninsula, but gained fame when he appeared to Christian warriors and gave inspiration to drive out the Moors.

- ❖ Twenty-two miracles are attributed to St. James, most of them occurring during the twelfth century.

- ❖ Pilgrimages to the site in Santiago started shortly after the miracles occurred and have continued to the present time.

- ❖ Today, the Camino is more popular than ever.

Tip #2

Know What to Take
and
What to Leave Behind

It does not take much strength to do things, but it requires great strength to decide on what to do.
Elbert Hubbard

Nothing is more difficult, and therefore more precious, than to be able to decide.
Napoleon Bonaparte

There are many decisions that will affect your journey. One of the most important is having what you need when you need it. You don't want to carry unnecessary things, or things you can buy locally.

Tip #2 – Know What to Take and What to Leave Behind

Many lists have been printed in books and put on the internet to suggest what is necessary for the trip. These are quite useful, but never complete as every traveler has unique needs that will alter the list. The time of year and the route chosen will also dictate what things should be taken or left behind. What is offered here is a generic list to be modified as needed.

You will need:

Footwear
Backpack
Something for sleeping
Fanny pack
Money belt
Clothes
Toiletries and grooming products

Medicines – prescriptions, glasses
Towel and washcloth
Guidebook
Sunglasses
Miscellaneous items

You might want:

Camera
Batteries
Extra clothes
Rain poncho
Makeup
Something from home
Spanish phrase book
Personal journal
First aid kit
Flashlight

Ear plugs
Neck cooler
Hat
Sleep mask
Watch
Air mattress/sleep pad
GPS (Global Positioning System)
PEG (Personal Energy Generator)
Cell Phone

Extras that make a difference:

Ziploc bags
Space-saver bags

Duct tape
Handiwipes

Leave at home:

Nightclothes	Hairdryer
Jewelry	Water bottle

What You Will Need

There are certain things that are essential for the trip, whether it is for the entire five hundred miles or only a portion of it. What follows is an explanation of why each of these things is essential. At least they were essential for me and for most of the people on the journey.

Footwear

Probably the most important thing for a five hundred mile walking trip is to have appropriate footwear. The type of footwear can vary widely. I saw everything from army boots to flip-flops, each of which provided varying degrees of comfort and successful use. Most of the guide books I had read before undertaking the trip advised travelers to get a good pair of hiking boots for the mountain trails and a pair of sandals to wear at the albergues in the evening. What I observed on the trail did not support this advice.

Most pilgrims who were going to get blisters got them during the first few days of walking. The reason they got blisters is because they were wearing shoes not adequately broken in. Buying a new pair of hiking boots and wearing them for a month or two before starting the journey is not enough. I spoke with people who had no problems with blisters during their "warm up" at home. However, when they started the actual trail and were walking all day long, up and down trails, the boots rubbed in places that had not been touched before and caused blisters. Many pilgrims bravely (or foolishly, depending on your viewpoint) continued walking until their feet were infected and a doctor had to be summoned.

One Irish lad, about a week into the journey, had walked until he could go no further. His blisters were so badly infected that it was painful to stand. The on-call doctor ordered him to soak his feet in antiseptic, take an oral antibiotic and rest for a couple days until walking would be more comfortable. However, his enthusiasm was not to be curbed and I saw him on the trail the next day wearing flip-flops. His walk was slow, every step looked painful and I wondered if he would make it. We ran into each other several times over the course of the Camino and he eventually made it all the way. Determination and will power played a large part in getting him to his destination. Had he had more suitable footwear to start, the journey might have been more enjoyable. I do not want to judge as I do not know what spiritual demons he was exorcising through his feet. Maybe that was his intent.

If you have no foot guilt and would like to traverse the entire Camino without foot problems, my advice is to wear a pair of shoes that you already own and have worn for at least several months. The shoes can be upgraded with new insoles, better socks and just for fun, new ties. The tried and true shoes will fare better than the new and improved. If you must purchase new shoes, do so as soon as possible and wear them as much as possible before leaving. Six months of constant wearing would help tremendously.

Today's footwear technology is light-years ahead of where it was even a decade ago. Comfortable, protective and attractive footgear can be purchased with a minimum investment. I took a pair of Asics running shoes and a pair of Teva sandals that I had been wearing for over a year. My husband wore his favorite New Balance 806 trail running shoes and a generic pair of flip-flops for the evenings. The trail running shoes had an excellent sole for the diverse trails we encountered. He walked with ease over many different surfaces. We both walked the entire 500 miles blister free.

I did have one foot problem at the beginning of the trip. The first two days out of St. Jean-Pie-de-Port is in the Pyrenees and required climbing for half of the day and descending the other half. The ascent was no problem, but on the descent my feet constantly slipped forward and my big toes kept continually bumping against my shoes. When it started feeling uncomfortable, I stopped and put on my Teva sandals so my toes would have nothing to bump against. My husband was horrified that I was walking in sandals, but for me they were quite comfortable. The sandals had excellent support and had been fully broken in before starting the journey.

The bumping of my toes in my shoes did, however, take its toll. It became uncomfortable to wear enclosed shoes. My husband looked on in dismay as I calmly took my Swiss Army knife and cut out the front part of the shoes and made my toes free from constraint. These were old shoes and I had no particular attachment to them. I saw them as a means to protect my feet and was planning to get rid of them at the end of the journey.

One concession we both made before starting the trip was to put new arch supports in both pairs of running shoes. There are varying degrees of quality in insertable supports. We went to a reliable outdoor gear shop and purchased Spenco supports. We bought a medium grade product that helped tired feet and allowed us to use the shoes we had already broken-in. Arch support products can also be custom made for your individual feet. These cost about a hundred dollars per pair and require a month or so for processing. If you have sufficient time and money, this could make your feet very happy.

There is debate about the type and quantity of sock(s). Many references advised wearing two pair of socks; one thin pair covered by one thicker pair. The logic is: with two pair of socks, any rubbing against the skin is minimized and blisters are avoided. My husband is a thin sock advocate and I usually prefer the thicker socks, so before leaving on the trip we each traded a pair of socks to try this technique. Both of us found it uncomfortable and readily switched back to our usual style. What we did do to enhance our sock experience was to splurge and buy expensive, ergonomically designed socks specifically for foot comfort. They come in both thin and thicker variety, so we were each able to retain our personal sock philosophy and gain additional comfort. These socks were purchased at an outdoor gear shop and range in price from about $10 to $25 a pair. We each found a medium priced style we liked and we both purchased two pair. Talk to a knowledgeable salesperson and they will explain the advantages of each type of sock. You can then find something that will suit your needs.

The sock purchase was the second smartest thing I did to avoid problems and make the journey pleasant. The socks hug and massage the feet, so that, at the end of the day my feet were tired, but not painful or aching. I did not realize just how comfortable they were until one day I resorted to a pair of normal, discount store socks I had brought along "just in case." I do not even remember why I deviated from my luxury sock program, but I found myself on the trail in ordinary socks. After only a couple of hours, my feet were complaining. Not being one to ignore body parts that start talking to me, I assessed the situation and was soon rummaging through my backpack for the luxury socks. Upon donning them, my feet immediate sent a "thank you" signal to my brain and I was able to complete the day's journey in comfort. My "just-in-case" socks went into the trash at the next albergue and my pack was a few ounces lighter.

I ended up walking most of the Camino in my luxury socks and Teva sandals. My feet sweat a lot and I do not like confining shoes. The sandals were one of the classic models that have good support and are lightweight. I carried my running shoes all the way to Santiago and ceremoniously threw them away. At my husband's suggestion, I put them on when the terrain looked rough. However, I ended up digging in my backpack and pulling out the sandals at some time during the day.   If I ever do this sort of thing again, I will take a good pair of sandals and three pair of luxury socks.

As a final note on footwear, use common sense. Do not purchase new shoes unless you can do so many months in advance and wear them daily in those intervening months. Do not change your comfort style, but add to it.   Try everything at home at least a few weeks before you plan to leave.   Your feet are your mode of transportation. Guard them and pamper them as you would your most valuable possessions. You will not regret it.

Those of you who are reading closely will notice that I stated that my sock purchase was the second smartest thing I purchased for the journey.   Read on to find out what the smartest thing was.

Backpack

Your backpack becomes your home while you are on the trail.   It houses all your possessions, and is your constant companion.   It can be your best friend or your worst enemy depending on how well it fits your body and walking style.   There are a myriad of manufacturers who make hundreds of different styles and sizes. The trick is to find the one that is just right for you.

When I originally started thinking about walking the Camino, I thought I could pare down the amount of things I would need and make do with a daypack I already owned. After all, one of the lessons to be learned was to prioritize things in life and only take what was really necessary. My husband convinced me I was not going to be entering the ascetic life of a nun or monk and the world of the twenty-first century did not require such sacrifice to be spiritual.   Spiritual issues aside, cultural norms require that a person undergo some grooming routines and clothe the body in an acceptable manner. I would need more room in my backpack.

My next backpack inspiration came when I saw an advertisement for a backpack with wheels! Wow! In level places I could take it off my back and pull it behind me. It seemed like the ideal combination and it was with the full intention of purchasing such a composite that my husband and I visited The Summit Hut, an outdoor gear store in Tucson, Arizona.

We were greeted by a young, enthusiastic and, it turns out, knowledgeable sales person, who greeted my inquiry into the virtues of a composite backpack with a look of concern and dismay. He discretely enquired about our upcoming trip and asked if I had considered any other alternatives. When the basics of the trip had been explained, he led us to a wall of backpacks, expertly sized me up and chose one from the wall for me to try on, all the while chatting about the various advantages of the different styles. Some were top loading, some had zippers down the side. Some had many pockets and compartments and some were like duffel bags with straps.

I was learning a lot about backpacks. The size of a backpack (small, medium or large) does not refer to the amount of things put in it, but to the size of the frame that will either hug your body with delight, if it is the right size, or inflict large amounts of pain if it is the wrong size. The first couple of packs I tried just did not feel comfortable, but then the magic happened. We had talked about pockets and compartments and he selected a pack that seemed to mould itself to my body. As I was marveling in the feeling, he was further adjusting the scores of straps and explaining the proper adjustment of each one to make it fit perfectly. I was beginning to have great respect for this young man.

He deepened my respect when he suggested I put some weight in the pack to see how it felt. The store had "pillows" of varying weight to be inserted to simulate how a particular backpack would ride on the body with that weight. He selected forty pounds of pillows and stuffed them comfortably in the pack. Forty pounds! I couldn't believe it. He then invited me to walk around the store for a while with the weight to see how it felt. It was not only a good sales technique for selling the pack, it was also a good sales technique for everything else in the store. At this point, the young man was my new messiah and I listened closely for any words of wisdom that issued forth concerning other products. (He was the one who introduced us to the marvelous socks.)

While I walked around the showroom feeling like I could conquer the world, the young shaman performed the same magic for my husband. My husband had an additional concern, as he had had an operation four years earlier that had fused two vertebrae in his neck. He was apprehensive about aggravating the condition by carrying weight. The young man was able to select a pack that put all weight on my husband's hips, and when properly adjusted, did not even touch or stress his neck area.

We now both had custom packs that would allow us each to carry forty pounds, if necessary. I was not planning to lug that much. My goal was twenty pounds, but it gave me an extra feeling of security to know I could carry more if the need arose.

The way the pack is loaded also makes a difference in how heavy it feels. As counter-intuitive as it sounds, the heavier items should go in the top, near the head, rather than on the bottom. With a good pack, this will distribute the weight to the hips and it will not seem heavy at all.

I can not go into all the pros and cons about specific backpacks. You should visit a reliable store that carries outdoor gear and latch on to a knowledgeable salesperson. Talk to this person and find out if the knowledge comes from personal experience or if it sounds like a sales pitch. Most good quality stores try to hire staff who actually engage in the activities they are promoting. This practice pays off for both the store and the customer. The sales person should be able to talk to you about what you want to do, any health restrictions you might have, and be able to fit you with a pack to fulfill your wants and not aggravate health issues.

The pack that works like a dream on one person can be a nightmare for another. Midway on the Camino, while we were waiting for an albergue to open, another pilgrim came up with the exact same pack I was using. "Don't you just love it!?!" I gushed, thinking he would have the same enthusiasm I did. His reply of "You've got to be kidding!" and his look of disdain told me all was not well in his corner of the backpack arena. This opened the door for him to tell us all about the back pain he was enduring and the stress on his shoulders and neck. A quick glance at his six foot stature compared to my five foot five told me he should not be wearing the same pack as I was. Further conversation revealed that he had wanted a small pack as he was not going to carry much weight. He either did not have a knowledgeable salesperson or he had ignored their advice.

Accepting sage advice and buying a well-fitting pack was the smartest thing I did for myself for the trip. But my newfound backpack guru was not quite finished. Read on for another important item and what we did about it.

Something for sleeping

The albergues along the Camino offer shelter and a bed. A plain bed. Sometimes with a pillow, sometimes without. Sometimes with covers, but most of the time without. So a pilgrim must come prepared to sleep comfortably. This means a sleeping bag and that is how we equipped ourselves for the trip.

I already had a sleeping bag from my time in the Peace Corps. It was several years old and a bit bulky and heavy by today's standards, but still comfortable and usable. I opted to use it and not spend money for a new one.

However, my husband did not have one, so while I was still looking around with forty pounds on my back, he started talking about a sleeping bag. Once again, talking with someone who knows the products can be quite enlightening. Our miracle worker salesperson did not disappoint. At the time we were engaged in this buying activity, most of the literature we had read talked about spending at least one night under the stars for various reasons: lack of space at the nearest albergue, getting caught between towns with an albergue and being exhausted or just wanting to go off the beaten path and spend some time with nature. The literature had said the temperature could dip to around freezing at night. My husband wanted something to keep him warm if we did have to sleep outside and would serve as a blanket or something he could crawl into and zip up for those cool nights we might spend in albergues.

The technological explosion that created our wonderful backpacks did not leave sleeping bags behind. They also come in sizes. There is no sense getting one too big because it will have added weight and every ounce counts when packing. One too small will limit movement and make sleeping uncomfortable. The content of new bags varies - from synthetic, which I have because of allergies, to the softest down, which my husband chose because it weighed less than a pound and is quite compact. His bag reduced to a small bundle about seven inches high and five inches across. By comparison, my bag of twenty years was about twice the size and weight.

There are various styles of bags, the most popular being the mummy bag which clings to the contours of the body. Some couples may choose a rectangular bag, to accommodate the two of them, which can be zipped together for cuddling on the trail. When separated they can be formed into two separate rectangular sleeping bags or two blankets. When used as a blanket it can be quite useful on the Camino. However we did not encounter any double beds when they might be put together. The closest thing is when two bunk beds are pushed side-by-side.

One thing we did not think about at the time, but that ended up bothering my husband on the trail was the zipper on the bag. On my bag the zipper goes from the tip of the toe to the top around the hood. It is a two way zipper and if my feet get hot I can reach down and unzip the bag from the bottom and stick my feet out while the rest of the zipper keeps the bag around me. The zipper in my husband's bag did not go all the way to his feet and did not have the two way zipping capabilities. Consequently, he was either in or out of his bag – nothing in between. Zipper style and length could be a consideration point when purchasing a bag.

To accompany our sleeping bag I also purchased a silk sleep sack to function as a sheet inside the bag. It is much easier to wash a silk sheet than it is to wash the entire sleeping bag and I did not want to go the entire time on the Camino without having clean sleeping materials. These sheets can be purchased inexpensively on EBay or in specialty stores for about $10 to $25 each. (Enter "Silk Sleep Sack" on EBay and you will get a list of vendors.) On many nights, this was all we needed for covers and we were the envy of pilgrims who had not thought of bringing one or had not known that they even existed. Each one only added about seven ounces to our pack, and could be put in the sleeping bag stuff sack with ease.

I did not know if pillows would be provided or not, but decided to take my own pillowcase for sanitary purposes. Again, silk is wonderful material for its compactness and its soothing quality next to your skin. I bought each of us a silk pillowcase for about five dollars each. When no pillows were provided, I simply put my extra clothes in the pillow case and had a makeshift pillow that worked just fine.

Our provisions of sleeping bags, silk sheets and silk pillowcases turned out to be a bit of overkill. We walked the Camino during the months of June and July and most of the time it was warm at night. At bedtime we would each crawl into our silk sheet and only pull the sleeping bag over us if the night grew cool. Sleeping in the same room with twenty or thirty people can generate a lot of warmth.

Since returning from our trip, I have thought about the need to have a sleeping bag. A flannel sheet would provide some warmth while not being as bulky as a sleeping bag. There are other alternatives which might also be better while still providing enough comfort in the night.

Fanny pack

A fanny pack is included under necessities because everyone had one. It functions as purse or carry bag and is packed with things for quick access. It makes shopping in the evenings easier. The backpack stays in the albergue, and the fanny pack can be used to carry money and small valuables safely. I carried my reading glasses, my camera, tissues, throat lozenges, lip balm, a bit of cash, my driver's license, and a credit card.

The fanny pack is put on first, and worn in front. The hip belt on the back pack can be clasped underneath the fanny pack.

Money belt

Under my clothes, I wore a money belt that contained my backup credit card, my passport and excess cash. This was purely a security measure. We did not encounter any problems during the entire trip, but along the way we heard rumors about some pilgrims being robbed. Alas, it probably does happen and there is no sense in inviting trouble by displaying valuables. There are many styles of money belts, and not all are actual belts. Some are worn around the neck. I feel more secure with something around my waist. Also it is more easily concealed than something around the neck.

Money belts or necklaces are made out of lightweight material. I again chose silk for its comfort. Some include plastic containers to hold a passport and insure it does not get wet from rain or sweat. Personally, I discarded the plastic, as passports are made from fairly durable material and they do dry adequately after being wet. The voice of experience is talking here.

Clothes

Put all the clothes you think you will need in a pile. Then take half of them away. What is left is closer to what you actually need. You need to be able to put on clean clothes for a day and have one extra set. That usually means two of everything. The time of year you will be walking and the route you decide to take will define the type of clothes necessary. For cooler weather, layer clothing that you otherwise would wear alone. Make each piece of clothing work for its spot in your backpack. If it cannot be worn for more than one purpose, consider substituting it with something else.

I inadvertently over packed and carried more clothing than I needed. There was one pair of shorts I did not wear the entire trip because it would have been difficult to wash and dry quickly. So here is a list of the clothing I actually used:

2 pair of shorts with built in underwear
2 tops to wear with the shorts
2 bras (for women)
2 pair underpants

1 pair long pants with zip off legs and many pockets
1 long sleeve pullover running top
1 long sleeve shirt with Velcro fasteners
2 pair of socks

The important thing about this list of clothes is the material each item was made from. I bought most of the items at a running store, so that the materials were lightweight, breathable, and could be washed by hand and dried quickly. The long pants took the longest time to dry, but even they dried in a few hours on sunny days. On cool days I would put on the long pants, one of the shorts tops, the long sleeve top and the long sleeve shirt. On the rare cold day, I may have shivered a bit as we started out, but within the hour I would start to shed clothes. We would take a break, pull off an article of clothing and put it back in the pack. By mid morning, I was usually down to the shorts top and long sleeve shirt with the legs zipped off my pants, so they effectively became shorts.

The exertion of walking every day creates warmth within the body, so unless you are very cold natured or you are planning to walk during the winter months, you will easily warm up as the day unfolds.

Toiletries and grooming products

This collection of items is the heaviest group in your backpack, so special attention should be put towards prioritizing what is really necessary. Here is a brief list of essential items:

Body soap	Dental floss
Shampoo	Nail brush
Deodorant	Emery board
Comb and/or brush	Bug repellant (general purpose)
Toothbrush	Bug repellant (bedbugs)
Toothpaste/tooth soap	Sunscreen

Facial cleanser (for women)	Tissues and toilet paper
Facial moisturizer (for women)	Shaving kit (complete kit for men, razor for women)
Body lotion	

You do not have to take enough of each item to last the entire trip. All of these things can be purchased along the way. Even though the Camino tradition is hundreds of years old, the trail goes through modern cities. Spain is a first world country, after all. You will not be traveling back in time. So unless you have a need for a specific brand sold only where you are living, these items can be replenished or replaced. Only pack enough to get you through a couple of weeks.

However, you may not be able to purchase every item in every little town you walk through. So it is a good idea to have some of the items with you at the start. Also, things like bug repellant and sun screen are rather expensive on the trail, so there is a balancing act when deciding how large a bottle to bring. But let's look at each item individually.

My husband and I both have dry skin and regularly use a liquid moisturizing **soap** at home. However, it is quite heavy to carry so we each took a bar of Dove soap. Originally, I put the soap in a travel soap holder, because it was damp from my morning wash, but that soon became cumbersome and I ditched the holder in favor of a ZipLoc bag. A problem arose with the moisture in the bag softening the soap and the bar was soon gone. I was able to find moisturizing bar soap in a local shop. I then changed my technique when packing the soap. Instead of just putting it in the ZipLoc bag, I would first get as much water off the bar as possible and then wrap it in my wash cloth and put it in the ZipLoc. The wash cloth absorbed the small amount of water still on the bar and preserved it better. When I took it out of the bag in the afternoon to shower, there was more of the bar left to use.

Towards the end of the trip, I abandoned using bar soap in favor of using a bit of **shampoo** to wash my body. This seemed to work well and gave me one less thing to carry. Shampoo, after all, is specialized soap.

Traveling with a companion can have weight advantages, as my husband and I shared the shampoo, and alternated who carried it. Not being aware of what might be available, we each had packed a bottle at the beginning of the trip. However, when we realized things could be easily replaced, we combined resources as they were used.

If you use a conditioner, it is to your advantage to try to find a shampoo and conditioner combination. It may not give your locks the same treatment, but you are going to be walking a trail all day long and not sitting in an office or doing your usual routine. Looking picture perfect is not necessary. Review **Tip #3** for some hair tips.

Everyone needs to use a **deodorant** and/or antiperspirant. It usually comes in a plastic container with a device for extruding the product which is spread on the underarms or other offending body part. The amount of time you will be on the Camino is brief and you will not need a complete container of deodorant. In an effort to keep the weight and volume of your pack down, the container can be dismantled, and only the deodorant is carried. This can be done only with solid deodorant. Liquid or cream will not work. To accomplish this, screw the mechanism at the bottom to extrude about one to one and a half inches of deodorant. Cut this off and place it in a small plastic bag or wrap it in a piece of Saran Wrap. Leave the container at home for when you return. The deodorant can be applied by using the plastic (bag or wrap) to hold it and spread it on. It is a little cumbersome at first, but you will get the hang of it and not be offending to your fellow pilgrims while keeping your pack weight down.

A **comb** is necessary for unruly locks and does not take up much space. Depending on the length of your hair, you may or may not need a

brush. If you do, consider getting a travel size or purse size one to take along.

Toothbrushes are universal and are available just about everywhere. If you normally use a battery powered or plug-in toothbrush, a return to the old fashioned type is just what you will need for this trip. There are also disposable toothbrushes (Wisp by Colgate) that contain toothpaste on the brush and have a small dental pick opposite the brush end. These do work well and will lighten your pack as you use and dispose of them. However, it may be cumbersome to take enough to last the entire journey.   If your dental hygiene is dependant on some special care, talk to your dentist about what might be done during the trip. Whatever you do, keep it simple.

American brands of **toothpaste** are also readily available and can be replenished along the way. I would recommend taking a travel size tube because it does not weigh too much or take up much space. Other alternatives to toothpaste are tooth powder or tooth soap. Both of these are lighter in weight, smaller in volume and do a great job of keeping your teeth pearly white. I use **tooth soap** and was able to put enough soap in a 35mm film container to last me the entire trip. Tooth soap looks like bar soap that has been roughly grated. Each shred of soap is enough for one brushing. You may find these products in health food stores in the US. I did not find anything like them in Spain. I buy tooth soap over the internet. Enter "tooth soap" in a search engine and you will be given several places where it can be purchased.

We took one container of **dental floss** and it was enough for both of us the entire trip.   If at all possible, take the brand you like from home. It may be available in larger cities, but I do not remember seeing it in the smaller stores in villages.

A **nail brush** is a multi-purpose object that I always take on trips. It performs the obvious function of keeping my nails clean and my cuticles in check and it can be used for any brushing activity that is needed.   I have used mine to get spots off my shoes, backpack, and clothing.   It can clean stubborn spots off dishes and pans.   And it can be discarded at the end of the trip.

Emery boards are good for keeping nails looking good.   On the trail my nails seem to break a lot, so I keep an emery board handy to file any rough edges.   They can be thrown away when worn out.

Depending on the time of year and the hours you plan on walking, **bug repellant** may or may not be necessary.   Bugs are more active in the early morning and late at night or when there is no breeze to blow them along. If you are wearing clothing that covers the body, repellant is only necessary around the face and hands.   Before the trip we had read conflicting reports about how bad the bugs were.   Rather than being caught off guard and attacked by some hungry insects, we decided to take repellant. We took two forms- a small bottle of liquid and repellant "bracelets" which could be worn and re-used.   Both were purchased at a discount store like Wal-Mart or Target.

We were lucky in our encounters with insects, as we did not have any bad incidents.   We wore our bracelets and they sufficed.   However, an encounter with malevolent insects is a definite trip spoiler, so I would recommend including some form of repellant.

In recent years **bedbugs** have become a problem. In 2008 there was a major infestation along the Camino and many albergues became infected. Bedbugs are extremely difficult to get rid of. As a pilgrim, the major concern is repelling them, not eradicating them.   As of this writing, there is no available repellant that is easily carried.   Most literature on bedbugs talks about how to get rid of them in a home with chemicals.

The best defense is to be aware of the problem and not stay in an establishment that is infested. Word travels fast along the Camino and when an infestation becomes known, albergues have been known to refuse lodging to a pilgrim who stayed at an infected site the night before. So always check your mattress before settling in and if you see anything suspicious, leave and find another place to stay.

If you find you have picked up a critter, there are steps you can take. They do not like extreme temperatures. Freezing will kill them, but that is not practical. The best thing to do on the trail is to completely disassemble your backpack's contents and leave everything in the hot sun for a few hours. Turn the items periodically, as bedbugs will try to hide in the shade.

Further research on the internet may prove useful, as new products are always emerging.

Sunscreen is a must, no matter what your skin type is. I got skin blisters on the back of my legs on a cloudy day. We were walking up a series of hills to the windmills after leaving Pamplona. I did not even think of applying sunscreen. The wind, combined with the sun's rays that got through the clouds put small blisters on my upper calves. I did not realize it until we were stopped and I was washing off the grime of the day. Luckily, it only caused discomfort for one night and I was able to avoid any further skin problems. I became a sunscreen junkie and applied it every morning before heading out. My husband followed suit and our diligence was repaid with skin that not only looked good, but felt good and healthy at the end of the journey. I would recommend at least an SPF 30 or higher depending on the sensitivity of your skin. This can be purchased en route in the larger cities. Pharmacies or supermarkets will carry it.

Most women have a favorite **facial cleanser** and **moisturizer**. If it is an American brand name, it probably will not be available along the trail. Or if it is, the price will be exorbitant. For this reason, I took enough of each of these products to last the entire trip. I advise other women to do the same.

We brought a small bottle of the **body lotion** from home. However, after starting to use the suntan lotion, the generic skin lotion was replaced by suntan lotion when it was used up.   Many brands of American body lotion and of course, European brands, can be found in supermarkets, pharmacies and general stores along the way.

Tissues and **toilet paper** turned out to be more of a necessity than I had imagined.   Most albergues provide toilet paper.   However, there were a few times when an albergue was overwhelmed with pilgrims and the toilet paper was quickly used up.   A black market economy is created among the pilgrims who brought their own and those who did not.   One begins estimating the number of squares or tissues that will be personally consumed before the next store is accessible before sharing any abundance with needy pilgrims.

And here I must broach a delicate subject: the use of tissues on the trail. There are many, many places on the Camino which are quite deserted and away from civilization. Nature will call and you will find yourself searching for just the right hiding place. Yes, you will urinate and defecate along the trail. Everyone leaves their DNA for posterity. And any bushy plant or large rock that conceals the ideal spot to squat also looked good to others. So there will probably be a collection of tissues left by others.   Tread carefully.

For ease of packing and use, I bought several purse size tissues packs to put in my backpack. I kept an open pack of tissues in my fanny pack for quick retrieval. My husband preferred to carry part of a roll of toilet tissue. Since men have the urinary advantage in the outdoors, he did not need to retrieve tissues as often as I did.   Both tissues and toilet paper are available at markets and supermarkets along the way.

Disposable **razors** and **shaving foam** are also available along the way. Bring travel size shaving foam and a couple of disposable razors from home to start the journey. Replace these in larger cities at supermarkets and in smaller cities in general stores.

Medicines – prescriptions, glasses

Any prescription medication should be kept in the bottle or package showing your name and the name of your doctor. We were not searched or asked about any of our medicines, but considering the consequences if a customs agent thinks you might have contraband, it is worth it to keep it in the pharmacy container. Customs officials coming back into the US are more stringent about questioning individuals concerning any suspicious pills.

Take sufficient quantities of all the prescription medication that you require. Your doctor can write a prescription for a period sufficient to last for the entire trip. It is also a good idea to check with your doctor about getting replacements in the event of lost luggage or theft. US prescriptions can not be filled in Spain. However, many prescription drugs in the US are over-the-counter in Spain. Make a list of your drugs, using the Latin name and what each is being taken for and keep it with you. Spanish pharmacists can help you replace lost medicines or may know of a substitute they can give you. They are in touch with doctors in the area who could write a prescription if necessary. Albergues, hotels and hostels have doctors on call at all hours.

It would be better to alert your doctor to the possibility of loss during your trip and have him/her aware of the situation. Your doctor can call your local pharmacy and have the prescription re-filled. A friend can pick it up (be sure to make the contingency plans in advance) and overnight it to you using one of the international carriers such as DHL,

UPS or FedEx. Having a plan in place before you go will make it much easier to recover should something happen to your medications.

Over-the-counter drugs and supplements should be taken in sufficient quantities for the entire trip. While aspirin, ibuprofen and a few other common pain relievers were available, most were not. If you have a favorite brand of aspirin or ibuprofen, take it, as the brands in Spain are different. Again, keep everything in its original bottle at least until you have cleared customs. No sense upsetting a customs agent who may think your daily vitamin resembles the latest recreational drug. It would be even more upsetting for you.

Undertaking a journey of 500 miles, or even part of it will put a strain on the body. Training for a few weeks or months before will help, but the actual event will still take a toll. I wanted to be prepared and had read conflicting advice about the availability of supplements. So I decided to take a supply of everything I thought my body might need. I took:

Ibuprofen for general aches and pains,
Potassium supplements for muscle cramps,
Daily vitamin for general health,
Chondroitin glucosamine supplements for joint stress,
Echinacea for general immune system support,
Vitamin B complex for stressful situations.

This was my personal choice, but I found it to be a good one. I took my supplements at night so they could repair the stress of the current day and prepare my body for the new venture in the morning. I was glad I had enough for the entire trip, because I did not find supplements like mine in any store. Review **Tip #7** for more information.

Although there were many days, especially at the beginning, when I was exhausted from walking and my muscles and joints were sending me warning signals, I did not get sick. I credit my supplement regimen with keeping my body in good condition.

My advice here is to review your supplemental intake and make sure you have enough with you. Talk to your health care provider about what you might need to undertake the walk.

If you wear **prescription glasses**, take a second pair in case of problems with your primary pair. My husband usually takes a pair with an older prescription that would see him through getting another current prescription. Also, make sure you take a glass case for storing your glasses while you sleep. There are no bedside tables in albergues. Glasses must have a sturdy holder to keep them safe. If you wear disposable **contacts** take enough for the entire trip plus a few extra. Follow the same process for emergency replacement that is used for medicines.

Towel and washcloth

Alburgues, with rare exceptions, do not furnish towels. You must bring your own. Towels take up a lot of room, especially big fluffy ones. For this trip, the practical towel is one which dries quickly and does not take up much room in a backpack. We ordered a camping towel from an outdoor catalog on the net. It is made of a synthetic blend to absorb water, yet wring out and be almost dry. A search on the internet for "camping towel" will yield many choices at reasonable prices. A Sham-Wow is another possibility.

For a washcloth, I cut a Handiwipe in half.   I took several of these for their multi-purpose use. When they showed signs of wear, I threw them out.

Guidebook

There were a few pilgrims we met who did not have a guidebook of any kind, but were letting the day and the path unfold for them at will. While this can make each day full of surprises, there is enough of the unknown in a trip like this and most pilgrims want to plan at least part of each day. A guidebook will help in creating this plan as well as providing information about the surrounding area. Most guidebooks are printed in four language versions: Spanish, French, German and English. The challenge is in finding a book you like in a language that you can understand.

Before embarking on this journey, I had ordered several books from Amazon that purported to be guidebooks for walking the Camino. None of the books I bought met my criteria of having adequate maps, having information about side trips, having sufficient illustrations of places, and being somewhat lightweight. I decided to wait until we got to our starting point to buy a book. I had read that books were in abundance on the Camino.

Depending on where the journey is started, there may or may not be guidebooks available. I had assumed they would be plentiful, but on the day we arrived in St. Jean-Pied-de-Port there were no books in English or Spanish, my second language.   We wanted to have something to tell us about the surrounding area and the exact path of the trail. There were two books available in French, so we chose the one with the better maps because the French was useless to us.

Since St. Jean Pied-de-Port is a popular starting point, a couple of items are provided for the pilgrim. One of these is a very basic map to the first stop of Roncesvalles, 27 kilometers away. Armed with this map, plus the French guidebook, we made our way on the initial part of the journey to Pamplona. The albergue in this wonderful city is located in the old part of the city and there were several bookstores with guidebooks for the Camino. However, there must have been many English speaking pilgrims who had recently started the journey, as there were still no books available in English. We chose one in Spanish and were able to use it all the way to Santiago. See **Appendix D** for particulars.

Since returning to the USA, I have attempted to find a copy of the book in English. I know it does exist because I encountered other pilgrims who did have the English version. So far, I have been unsuccessful. Internet bookstores, such as Amazon do not carry it, even in their European branch. My advice for the traveler is to get as much information off the internet before leaving in case there is a problem locating a book upon arrival. If you are not flying into a city directly on the Camino, try to find a book you like in the city you land in. When shopping for a book, the more information it has about the actual trail, the better off you will be. The few times we were unsure of a road to be taken the problem was resolved by studying the map in our book.

The criteria for choosing a book will vary from person to person, but in general the following guidelines may be useful:

> Maps which show enough detail for the pilgrim, depending on the mode of transport. This means there should be enough landmarks shown so a walker can distinguish which branch to take. A pilgrim on a bicycle or horse will have different landmarks and in many cases will take different paths. Travel by auto is completely different. Make sure the book you choose is for the mode of transport you are using.

> Illustrations and write-ups of interesting things along the path. If you are on a time schedule and have no interest in visiting some of the fascinating places along the Camino, there are books with JUST maps. I found the journey is much richer when one has a history of the area.

> Charts which show elevation. The path ascends and descends the entire journey. The elevation can make a difference in the number of kilometers traveled in a day. It was much easier to plan when we knew how strenuous the walk would be on a given day. Some albergues within 200 kilometers of Santiago have such maps and will give them out at a nominal fee per copy or even free.

> Indications of where albergues, bus stations, camping, tourist offices and points of interest are located. The more options you are aware of, the more choices you will have.

Sunglasses

Most days were sunny enough for sunglasses at least part of the day. Take a pair you are comfortable wearing. If they break, they can be replaced in larger cities and towns. Smaller towns and villages probably will not have them.

Miscellaneous Items

There are a few things that don't fall into any category but are indispensable on the trail. Included are:

Clothes pins
Clothes line
Safety pins
Swiss Army knife
Lip balm
Throat lozenges
Soap for washing clothes
Flat sink plug

Most albergues furnish clothes lines, but not clothes pins. If you don't want your clothes blowing away, take eight to ten clothes pins. We forgot these and purchased them early on the trail. They turned out to be very handy. We also had a plastic clothes line about six feet long with suction cups at each end. Although the suction cups did not work well when there was any amount of weight on the line, we were able to secure it using the loops that held the suction cups. It was used on the few occasions when no clothes line was provided and also doubled as material for tying things.

Safety pins serve so many purposes. When we did not have enough clothes pins, we used safety pins. If our socks did not dry on the line, we used safety pins to pin them to the bottom of the top bunk. By morning they were dry. A safety pin replaced a lost button on my long pants. A safety pin can hold still-wet socks to a backpack, and they dry as you walk. There are a hundred other uses possible, so take along several of differing sizes.

My Swiss Army knife contains a pair of scissors, a nail file, a corkscrew and a small saw as well as an assortment of blades. It always comes in handy. If you do not already have one, I would buy one before you leave. I am sure they can be found in the larger cities, but it would take some searching to locate the right store. If you take it with you, make sure you put it in your checked baggage or it will be confiscated.

Lip balm will keep your lips from chaffing or chapping and is readily available along the trail. This will go a long way to keep you looking like a civilized human and not someone who has been in the bush for months (even though you may feel that way).

Throat lozenges will keep you from constantly clearing your throat when it gets dry. They will also soothe a scratchy throat and ward off a sore throat. Halls is a common available brand. If you have a favorite brand, take it with you.

If you are like most pilgrims, you will be washing clothes daily.   You will need laundry detergent to wash them.   Powered or liquid detergent is available just as it is in the US, but there is also another alternative which is much more sensible for use on the trail. It is bar soap for laundry made especially for hand washing.   It can be purchased at supermarkets and general stores. It is a rather large bar, about five inches by two inches by an inch and a half.   In smaller stores, you can even purchase half a bar so you do not have to carry as much.   Ask for soap to wash clothes by hand (jabón para lavar ropa a mano).

Most sinks in albergues do not have stoppers. To fill the sink with water, you will need something to stuff down the hole.   The best thing to have is an inexpensive flat plug. Because it is flat and about five inches in diameter, it works on any size drain, either for the bathrooms or for the laundry. They can be purchased in most hardware or discount stores in the US. They are harder to find on the trail, so purchase this before you go.

What You Might Want

Everyone has different reasons for taking the journey along the Camino. Individual interests will also dictate what has priority in your backpack. What follows is a general list of items that were useful to me. Pick and choose for your interests and weight in your backpack.

I cannot fathom going on any trip without a **camera**.   The memories from pictures keep the trip alive for many years.   Advances in digital photography have made it so easy to take many pictures and not have to carry rolls of film to be developed. If you do not already have a digital camera, this might be the time to buy one. The small size of most cameras makes them easy to carry in a fanny pack or pocket. Pictures can be viewed immediately, so if a picture is not just the way you want it, it can be re-taken. There is no waiting for development of film and the possible disappointment of having no opportunity to re-shoot the picture can be avoided.

One consideration for a digital camera is the picture capacity before downloading to a computer. A camera which uses flash cards can make the number of possible pictures approach infinity. There are camera stores in the larger cities that sell flash cards to fit all types of digital cameras. Thirty-five millimeter film is also available.

I became so enchanted with all the things we saw along the way that I took over 2500 digital pictures. Upon returning home, I was able to pare the number down to a couple hundred of the best and most meaningful.

A digital camera must have **batteries**. Luckily, this is not a problem. Batteries are available virtually everywhere along the Camino, in big and small towns. Supermarkets and general stores virtually always carry them. Being a cautious person, and not wanting to be caught with dead batteries and wanting to take a picture, I always kept a fresh set in my backpack in case the batteries in my camera were depleted while in the countryside. Each time I replaced the batteries in the camera, I would buy a fresh set in the next town. This worked well for me and I went through about four sets of batteries over the length of the Camino.

Don't bother with rechargeable batteries. To use them effectively, you would need access to a plug at the albergue in the evening. Plugs are rare and are quickly claimed by pilgrims with dead cell phones.

It becomes boring wearing the **same clothes** day after day. Toward the end of the journey, I longed for something different to wear. The constant wearing and washing of the same two pair of shorts and tops had caused the material to become thinner and frayed around the seams. I did have one pair of shorts that I did not wear because they were of heavier material and would be harder to wash and dry. I saved them to wear in Santiago. It was a gift I gave to myself upon the completion of my journey.

The weight and space of extra pieces of clothing will have to be compared with the luxury of having something different to wear along the trail or in Santiago. It is possible to replace clothing along the trail. Larger cities do have outdoor gear stores where comparable clothing can be purchased. There are also many, many department and clothing stores where any style of clothing can be purchased. One only has to take time to locate and shop for whatever is desired.

Another alternative is to send any needed items, clothing or otherwise, to the General Delivery in cities on your route. This would require some advance planning, but would allow extra, luxury, or just replenishment of items along the way without extra time shopping. See **Tip #4** for more information on how to do this.

The time of year will determine the weather and how many rainy days you might have. We encountered only three during June and July. We were very happy that we had our **rain ponchos** on those days. Nothing would be worse than having your entire pack get wet. We saw other pilgrims with different degrees of rain protection, from plastic garbage bags to rain gear with a poncho and rain pants. We chose to take old ponchos purchased on a trip to Disney World. The bright yellow ponchos with Mickey Mouse on the back were a source of amusement to a few local children along the way.

When shopping for rain gear, look for something large enough to also cover your back pack, but will pack as small as possible and be lightweight.   There are places on the internet that will sell a wide range of products.

Most women who made the five hundred mile journey did so without **makeup**. As we got closer to Santiago, we encountered pilgrims with more and more amenities and one of these was makeup for women. Take whatever you need to feel comfortable, but be aware that you will be putting on the makeup in a common bathroom and it does add extra weight to the backpack.   If you are only walking part of the five hundred miles, then the extra weight may be well worth it.

I included a "**something from home**" category for pilgrims who would be on the journey alone or for a long time.   This "something" can be a picture, an object or something that will give comfort on trying days. There are times when every pilgrim is tired, frustrated and wondering why the Camino sounded so intriguing at the onset.   Something from home will bring personal reinforcement and allow even the most upset pilgrim to get back in a better frame of mind.

Many pilgrims write a daily **journal** about their adventure.   Doing so can bring many benefits.   It will be a permanent keepsake of the travel. It can provide insight into things experienced on the trip.   It can also provide relief from frustration or upsets that can occur during the day. When entering an albergue in the afternoon, it was not unusual to see several pilgrims engrossed in writing in their journals.   My husband and I both kept a journal.

When searching for the blank journal to take along, consider weight as well as beauty. I had originally picked out a beautiful leather bound book because I thought would make an esthetically lovely memento. However, it was heavy.   Upon reflection, I finally decided on a spiral book given to me by a good friend.   It was much lighter and still something I cherish.

Do not forget to include a pen that can be easily attached to the journal or kept in the fanny pack for quick access.

The journey across northern Spain will be much more enjoyable if you can converse with the local people. If you do not know any **Spanish**, take along a phrase book to help you order food in restaurants, ask for directions, and purchase necessities along the way. Your effort in procuring one will be rewarded many times over. Even if you cannot pronounce words correctly, and must read phrases directly from the book, the effort you make will be greatly appreciated by your hosts. They will be much more receptive and helpful to pilgrims who try to speak their language. This was aptly illustrated to us one day.

We were sitting in a small establishment, eating our midday sandwich which we had just purchased. We were tired and took longer than usual eating, enjoying the rest. During this time, several pilgrims came and went. The proprietor was the only one working, and in between customers, he was carrying on a conversation with what appeared to be a local man. At one point a German couple came in. They spoke no Spanish and made no attempt to try, but rather asked if anyone spoke German. When no one responded in the affirmative, the couple attempted to order food. I was not sure what they wanted and neither was the proprietor. They became frustrated and left. After they had left, the proprietor shook his head in dismay and commented to his friend that he thought pilgrims should at least learn a few words of Spanish so they could communicate. His friend concurred and they had a lively conversation about pilgrims who come through the area and expect the locals to be able to speak their language.

When shopping for a phrase or travel book, make sure you get one for Spanish in Spain, also known as Castilian Spanish. Many phrases and words used are different from Mexican or Latin American Spanish. Lonely Planet (http://lonelyplanet.com) publishes a small book of Castilian Spanish that easily fits in a pocket or fanny pack for quick reference. A little study before the trip and a little effort along the way will be greatly rewarded.

No one wants to think about anything bad happening along the way, but accidents do happen. A few things in a small **first aid kit** can make big difference when out on the trail. You might want to take:

Band aids
Moleskin for blisters
Antiseptic cream
Elastic bandage for pulled or tired muscles

All of these things can be purchased at pharmacies along the trail. However, they may not be available at the exact point you need them. I would advise bringing them from home. When my husband pulled a leg muscle, he had to walk several miles to the next town before we could find an elastic bandage. I also had to go to several pharmacies before I found one.   Pharmacies quickly sell out of things commonly needed by pilgrims. One additional delight, unavailable in the US, is an ibuprofen cream that can be rubbed directly into sore muscles.   It worked wonders at keeping the aches away from leg muscles and feet. Ask for it at any pharmacy in Spain.

A small **flashlight** can come in handy for many things.   I found one with a high-intensity bulb that is only about two inches long and about a half inch in diameter. It gives sufficient light to walk along a dark pathway at night. I also used it a couple of times to find my way to the toilet in the middle of the night when I had to maneuver through dark hallways. This particular flashlight was so small it only added a few ounces to my pack. I probably could have done without it, so this item will be a personal preference. If you decide you want one along the way, there are only a few places that carried a very small one. We saw plenty of standard size ones in the larger cities. Better to bring this from home.

If you are a light sleeper, **ear plugs** may be for you. However, buy them before you leave home, as there were several pilgrims who were searching for them, and I do not know of anyone who was successful. I had taken about 10 disposable ones and found I did not need them, so I passed them on to others. Research this before you leave and find a style to suit you.

"**Neck coolers**" are sometimes called cooling headwear. I was so glad I had one. They are pieces of cotton sewn into a tube with "magic" grains of chemicals within the tube. When it is soaked in water, these grains of chemicals absorb the water and swell up. You can then place this around your neck like a bandana and the water will keep you cool. When it dries out, it weighs practically nothing, so it is easy to transport until it is needed. The only disadvantage is that it takes a few hours of soaking to swell up properly for cooling. Here is where my Ziploc bags came in handy again. I filled one with water and put the neck cooler in it when I went to bed before an upcoming hot day. In the morning it was ready to use. I discarded the excess water in the bag and I was ready to go. It really does keep the body temperature down when the sun is brutal, such as between Burgos and León.

To get one, go to an outdoor store or even some drugstores. WalMart occasionally has them in the sporting goods department. If you can not find them on your own, ask a clerk for the neck cooler "thingies" that hold water and keep you cool. A knowledgeable sales clerk will lead you right to them. I also found an array of products on the www.blubandoo.com website.

Another method for fighting the sun is to have a **hat** of some sort. The right hat can also be good for repelling rain and shading your eyes. Outdoor gear stores have a variety of styles and you can be fashionable as well as comfortable. Buy one that folds in a suitcase and does not weigh much. While on the trail, there are various places where they can be purchased, however, you will have to hunt in the larger cities to find the right stores.

If light bothers you while you sleep, you might consider taking a **sleep mask**. Some of the albergues have lights outside the windows or in the rooms for safety. A mask is lightweight and will not add much to your pack, but buy before you go. I doubt if one would be readily available along the trail.

Not everyone had a **watch**. Some pilgrims wanted to be free of timekeeping and set their travels according to the sun. If you choose to wear a watch, you might consider a sports watch with a light so you can discretely tell the time in darkened albergues.

While planning for my trip, I was still under the belief that I would probably spend at least one night under the stars. A sleeping bag provides warmth, but no cushioning, so I carried a cheap **air mattress** which could give some separation between me and the cold, damp earth if sleeping outside. I never used it, as there was no lack of places to stay. If you plan to sleep outside, take something like this along. Otherwise, it was an extra weight that I would not have taken if I had been aware of the number of albergues available.

Technology has come a long way and many cell phones have a **GPS** unit. There are even specific applications for the Camino. The disadvantage of carrying a cell phone or any electronic gear is the scarcity of electrical plugs for recharging batteries.

As of this writing the PEG or **Personal Energy Generator** has just become available. It promises to be a boon to pilgrims who want to carry cell phones and small electronic items as they will be able to keep them charged as they walk. See http://greennpower.com/ for more information.

Extras That Make a Difference

Sometimes the way things are packed can make a difference. We used the products listed below to make packing more organized.

Ziploc bags in a variety of sizes were used to organize and compartmentalize small objects. It also kept all these items from getting wet, or in the case of bar soap, kept the wet inside. Larger bags held damp towels and wash cloths. We carried a few extra bags because they did wear out on the trail from frequent opening and closing.

All clothes were kept in **Space-Saver bags**. Yes, these are the bags advertised on late night television and in Sunday newspaper magazines. They really do work and compressed our clothes so they fit more comfortably in the backpack. We ordered the travel sizes and each of us had three bags. One bag had my long pants, long sleeve pullover, and extra socks. Another had the shorts, top, socks and bra that I was not wearing. The third had the extra shorts and top saved for wear in Santiago. The bags not only compressed the clothes, but also kept them dry.

Ask any man and he will tell you that **duct tape** is indispensable. It can prove itself on the trail by mending tears in backpacks, keeping shoes or sandals together or just keeping things attached. We did not take a full roll of tape, but rather wrapped about a yard or two around a pencil for easy access.

A pack of **Handiwipes** was, well, handy. They were used as wash clothes, an extra towel and a clean up cloth. When they showed signs of wear, I threw them away. I took my supply with me and did not see them in stores along the way.

Things to Leave at Home

I mistakenly thought I would use a **nightgown**. That idea lasted one night. When sleeping in a room with up to one hundred people, any sense of privacy is lost. In such a large gathering, or even in a small room with four to six people, they are strangers and one usually does not change clothes in front of strangers. In the morning, if you are wearing some sort of sleepwear, you will have to gather your day clothes, and stand in line to the bathroom to change. Everyone is usually in a hurry to be out on the road and excessive time in the bathroom is met with scowls from other pilgrims.

The solution to the nightwear dilemma is to sleep in the clothes you will wear on the road the next day. This keeps the time necessary for grooming in the morning to a minimum. Once we got into the rhythm of the road, this made a lot of sense. We could wake, put on shoes, amble to bathroom, wash our faces, brush our teeth and hair, and be on our way. As the clothes were of a material to shed wrinkles, we looked fresh in the morning. At least, as fresh as everyone else on the trail.

Do not take any excessive **jewelry**. It could be stolen and it just is not necessary. Rings, earrings and necklaces that are constantly worn are the best choices. But these are still subject to loss, so weigh the risk carefully. Leave all other jewelry at home.

If at all possible, leave the **cell phone** at home. Or only carry it to turn on in emergencies. Most albergues do not have a place to charge it in the evenings, and those few places where electrical plugs are available will be fought over by everyone who wants to charge their phone. Bring a Personal Energy Generator to charge you phone as you walk. As we got within one hundred kilometers of Santiago, we did see some people talking on cell phones as they walked. If you must be in touch with family or friends, just be aware of the restrictions for keeping the phone charged. Some pilgrims used their phones for alarm clocks and woke everyone in the albergue. See **Tip #6** for more information on this sensitive issue.

I do not remember any albergues with an electrical plug in the bathroom where a **hairdryer** might be used. Leave it at home. Read **Tip #4** for suggestions on hair care.

You do not need a specialized **water bottle**. Bottled water originally came from Europe and all places, big and small had bottles of water available for purchase. We bought a small bottle of water in Saint Jean Pied-de-Port and filled it up as we went along. There are fountains with drinkable water all along the way. However, with the current emphasis on recycling, or lack thereof, it might make sense to carry your own bottle and not purchase more plastic that will go into a landfill. Your decision.

Tip #2 Takeaways

❖ There are some basic items that all pilgrims should have.

❖ Modern technology can aid the pilgrim and make the trip more comfortable.

❖ Some things are best left at home.

Tip #3

Know How to Set Expectations and Goals

You are never too old to set another goal or to dream a new dream.
Les Brown

We tend to get what we expect.
Norman Vincent Peale

The thing about expectations is that they can ruin a perfectly good experience. If expectations are open, then a whole new world is revealed.

Tip #3 – Know How to set Expectations and Goals

For a journey like this, one must be ready physically, mentally, emotionally and for this particular journey, spiritually. There are also a few logistical things to address. There is planning to be done on many fronts and many things to arrange. The more you know before you leave for the trip, the better prepared you will be for any delays or unexpected events.

Expectations play a major role in the experience of any journey. Daily reality checks during the journey help bring expectations into manifestation. One of the best ways to make sure you accomplish your goals for the trip is to have reasonable expectations to start. There are several ways to set your expectations and goals.

Physical Expectations and Preparation

The most constraining factor, especially for non-Europeans, may turn out to be time. The more time spent on the Camino, the better. You will be able to see more things and your spirit can be away from the work-a-day world and get into the mindset of a pilgrim.

The traditional Camino, starting in Saint Jean Pied-de-Port and ending in Santiago, traverses 500 miles. There are many books and web sites that advocate navigating this distance in thirty days. This means about seventeen miles every day. This can be very difficult for anyone who is not in top physical condition. It will also limit side trips and other activities, as all the time will be spent on the road walking. Take a realistic look at how much time you will be able to spend on the trip. If you have two weeks vacation, and you will be coming from someplace outside Europe, you will likely only have about nine to ten days traveling on the Camino. It takes time to fly into Spain and get to the desired starting point for walking.

Many Europeans walk the Camino in stages, taking their two week vacation, going to a predefined starting point and walking for two weeks. The next year they start at the point where they stopped the previous year and continue the journey. I met several people who were doing the Camino this way and they found advantages to this method. They were able to take their time and take in extra side trips to interesting places. By walking just a section at a time, the spirit of the Camino was kept alive all year long. There was a feeling of anticipation for the upcoming year and satisfaction and accomplishment for what had been experienced in the years past. Several people who were doing this considered this the superior way to assimilate the Camino experience.

Of course, Europeans can get to the Camino quickly. If you will be coming from a distance, factor in a day or two to recover from jet lag and to get to your starting point. Then figure the number of days you will have to devote to walking. If it is not at least a month, then consider walking only part. It does not have to be a sequential part of the Camino, all near Santiago. If you want to start in Pamplona, but do not have the time to walk the complete journey from there, you can walk part of it, catch a bus for a few miles, and then walk again. You can do this repeatedly and only walk the easier or more comfortable parts. However, if your goal is to have a Compostela certificate, then you must walk the last 100 kilometers into Santiago. Because of this, many pilgrims start in the town of Sarria, which is just over the 100 kilometer mark.

Once you have figured out how much time you have, you can calculate the distance you want to walk each day. Let's say you plan to walk 15 miles each day to visit interesting places or to complete your requirements for the Compostela or for your own personal goal. Get a map of your home city. Plot out a course of 15 miles that will take you from your own front door and back again. Pick a pleasant day and go and walk the course. Do not worry about carrying a backpack the first time you do this. This is a test to see what you need to do to be ready to walk the Camino. Get up at a comfortable time, take a bottle of water and start walking. It is a good idea to plot the course to pass by some restaurants so you can stop to rest a bit, and get something to eat along the way. Evaluate how you feel at several points during your walking time. This will tell you how much work you may have to do before leaving. If you cannot comfortably walk the miles, set up a walking regimen to get yourself in physical shape for the trip. Or consider walking less each day.

You probably chose a relatively flat test route. It is a good test for the central part of the journey between Burgos and Leon, which is flat and, in the summertime, hot. However, many other areas have ups and downs that can have you huffing and puffing in no time. So, to prepare for a walk with inclines, find a place in your city that has some hills and try walking up and down for the distance you plan to walk each day. If you live in a city without hills, find a public building with a stairway and practice going up and down several flights of stairs to simulate the distance you want to go. Start out gradually, as this can be quite intense. If you belong to a gym, you can exercise on the stair-step to get your legs in shape. But remember, a half hour work out at the gym is not the same as walking all day long. Try to do several half-hour workouts with rest periods in between.

If you do not have the time to walk your required distance during your normal day, try running about three miles without stopping. This will give your body an overall workout and strengthen the muscles in your legs. It will also simulate the energy and fitness level needed to walk 15 miles.

If you already have a physical routine, wonderful! What keeps us in shape for everyday life is different from walking several miles every day. If you were quite tired after your test walk, that should tell you that you need to repeat it several times before leaving for Spain.

Repeat it until it feels good and you do not tire. Then get out your backpack. Start with about 5 pounds and add a little weight each time you walk until you are carrying the weight you expect to have on the Camino. Do this routine for at least six months before you are to leave. Make sure you have walked with your anticipated weight for at least a month. Then, stop all training about three days before you are to leave. Give your body time to rest immediately before leaving so it can recover from the strain you have been putting yourself through.

While you are doing all this physical activity, you should be wearing the shoes you plan to take with you. This will help get them, and you, into top condition. When you start carrying weight, use the backpack you will use on the Camino. Add weight in increments, as what seems light early in the morning, can seem like a ton in the afternoon after walking all day.

If you can, vary your routine. One day you walk the planned distance, another day you work out in the gym and another day you climb stairs. When you are walking, chose a hot day, a cold day, a dry day and a wet day. You will experience all types of weather and will know what you need to be comfortable in each circumstance. One day, walk on flat ground, the next day walk up hills. Walk on concrete sidewalks, walk on rough gravel and walk on hiking trails. If you can, walk in dry and not so dry creek beds. Walk in mud. You will encounter all these conditions. As you are discovering how you react to the different environments, take note of what might make them more bearable, such as rain gear, better shoes, lighter or heavier clothing and so on. As you realize these things, write down any needed supplies and buy them before leaving.

Before starting any new physical endeavor, it is a good idea to check with your doctor. This is the perfect time for a checkup and a physical. Your doctor can also advise you concerning appropriate training activities for your age and physical condition.

Another good physical practice for getting in shape is either yoga or tai chi. Both of these practices involve stretching and toning muscles. If you have never tried either of these, there are some very good DVDs for beginners that can be purchased at a reasonable price. Most cities have classes with personal instruction. Knowing a couple of good stretching techniques can prevent muscle cramps. Yoga can help with relaxation for winding down and sleeping in unfamiliar beds. And it can give you needed energy in the morning to start your day.

If you have friends who are runners or cyclists, they have a stretching routine they follow before going out for their runs. Find out what they do and incorporate some stretches in your physical routine. Also, many cities have running clubs or stores selling running equipment and clothing. These locations may also be able to give you information about stretching exercises.

One thing I did not anticipate was the accumulation of fatigue. When we started the journey, we were full of energy and completed our daily planned distance with relative ease. This is not to say it was easy. There were times, especially on some of the inclines, that I would literally walk 15 paces, stop to catch my breath, continue for another 15, stop again, and so on until I reached the crest of the hill I was on. I was not alone in this little "dance," as other pilgrims were doing the same. You do what you have to do to cover the distance. As we were nearing Santiago after about five weeks of walking, we were fatigued more often. Even though the path was relatively flat and easy walking at this point, we were still quite tired after the day's walk. Because we had some extra time, we walked fewer kilometers each day. Pilgrims who were just starting were full of energy and quickly passed us on the trail. We also took a couple of rest days when we found a nice city and a private albergue and we lounged around for a day or so. This provided a break and rejuvenated our bodies and spirits. Listen to your body and give it what it needs.

We had trained for about six months before leaving on the journey. There is a steep hill near our apartment and we started out walking up the hill. The first time we did it, I had to stop frequently. After climbing the hill several times, I was able to walk up it without stopping. I then started carrying some weight, until I could comfortably carry the twenty pounds I was planning to take. I tried to make the walk once or twice each week during the six months before leaving. As the departure date grew near, I walked it more often. It took about an hour to walk up and back covering a distance of about three miles round trip. In retrospect, I would have been in better shape if I had walked up and down the hill for the distance we had planned to travel each day. I would have had better stamina for walking all day.

As you are going through your physical training, take frequent reality checks. Can you easily walk the distance you have planned? If not, increase your training or decrease planned distance. Do you have enough time before you leave to get an appropriate amount of training done? If not, adjust your expectations of the distance to be walked or change the terrain you choose to travel so you will be walking on easier paths. Can you comfortably carry the weight of the items you plan to take? If not, increase training or decrease this weight. Above all, use common sense. The more realistic your distance expectations are the more likely you will be to achieve them.

A physical concern that does not involve training, but does involve planning is a suitable hairdo. I wear my hair short to medium length and my daily routine involves a hairdryer and a brush to style it and hairspray to help keep it in place. I knew I would be going to a place without hairdryers and I did not want to look unkempt. I was unsure if a mirror would be available. I did not know if I would be sleeping in the open and getting up to walk without the benefit of running water or other modern conveniences.

To solve this, I made an appointment at my beauty shop for the day before we were to leave. If my hair turned out to be unattractive, none of my friends would see me. My hairdresser came up with a wonderful hairdo that was easy to care for and looked presentable. I explained to her where I was going and that I would not have the usual conveniences to use on a daily basis. She cut it shorter than usual, but gave it lots of texturing. It practically combed itself and fell easily into place. The cut lasted for a little over a month. During our pilgrimage, we took a rest day in the lovely city of Sarria and I inquired about beauty shops near the albergue. There were several just a few blocks away. The recommended one was just off the Camino at the bottom of the hill when coming into town. I do not remember the name, but you can find it if you, too, need a haircut at this point. The hairdresser there was curious when I told him that my husband and I were walking the Camino. Apparently, not that many pilgrims get haircuts along the way. I again explained my problem with lack of conveniences and he was able to replicate my original hairdo. When I entered Santiago about ten days later, I felt good physically from the walk and I looked good too.

My husband wears his hair in a pony tail, so his hairdo was easy to work with. He made sure he had plenty of hair rubber bands with him. We did see them for sale along the way, so if your hair grows and you want to pull it back in a pony tail, you can find hair rubber bands and all hair care products in the larger cities.

We met a couple of pilgrims who went to the extreme and shaved their head for the journey. They, too, had wondered about the facilities and decided to take this measure to alleviate any problem with hair care. One of these pilgrims was a woman, and we met her just as her hair was starting to grow out to about a half inch. She wore a hat most of the time, so her very short hairdo was not evident.

Plan to cut your hair or let it grow, but figure out something comfortable. All albergues have bathrooms with some kind of mirror for grooming, running water for bathing and washing hair. Beyond that, you need to make your own preparations for your own style.

Not being ready for the physical demands of the Camino can ruin the trip. Ill-preparedness can bring about blisters, illness and disappointment. Be realistic. Start physical training at least six months before the planned trip, listen to your body when it complains and adjust your expectations or training accordingly.

Mental Expectations and Preparation

The more you know about something, the less you will be surprised if something unexpected occurs. In other words, if you are familiar, at least intellectually with Spain, the Camino and its history, the cultures you pass through and a bit of the language, then the reality of any unpleasant situations will be easier for you to deal with. So the mental preparation for the trip involves going back to school.

This process can also help you define your trip more precisely. As you find out about the country, culture, history and language, some things will appeal to you more than others. Concentrate on them and take in as much as you can. Visit your local library and discover the history of the region. Sign up at a local community college or university and take a Spanish class. Many schools offer summer classes in "traveler's Spanish," which can give you the basics to communicate needs. Do internet searches on all of the topics that interest you and read, read, read. Absorb as much as possible. As you discover things, you will find new ideas and questions arising.

Read books by people who have traveled the Camino in the past. There are many interesting novels and travel logs. Even though these trips may have been done a while ago, they will give you perspective.

Go on line to Amazon, Barnes and Nobel, Borders, or any book store and do a search for "Spain" or "Camino de Santiago" and a list of books will appear. Take a look at some of the books and links to other, similar books.

The book that has probably inspired the most people is "The Camino, A Journey of The Spirit" by Shirley MacLaine. It is an account of her experiences walking the Camino in 1994. A lot has changed since she was there, but her insights are unique and interesting. We met people from many different countries who had read her book in their native language and it had stimulated them to find out more and to eventually walk their own path on the Camino. Most people thought some of the happenings in Shirley's book were a little "far out," but nevertheless it started the process for them. This book piqued my curiosity and started me on my Camino.

Another noteworthy book is "The Pilgrimage" by Paulo Coehlo. This is a novel about a pilgrim which is quite interesting from the aspect of reading *between* the lines as the pilgrim grows spiritually and understands more about himself and his place in the world. The book also introduces several rituals that the pilgrim performs at different stages of the trip. I do not know if these were entirely made up by Coehlo or if there is some basis for them, but I found some of them to be quite beneficial. Many of the rituals are a form of meditation, and I practiced some of them as I went along the trail.

A good travel book can also be invaluable. Here I am talking about a general travel book and not necessarily one about the Camino. Many publishers have excellent guides that give information about getting to Spain and to a starting point on the Camino. As of this writing, travelers from the United States do not need a visa in advance. A traveler may stay in Spain for up to 90 days without a formal visa. Your passport should be valid for at least three months longer than the planned departure date from Spain. If you plan to stay longer, check with the Spanish consulate in Washington, DC for the procedure. For travelers who overstay the free visa period, there is possible jail time before being deported.

The US government also has a lot of available information about other countries. They publish a page of background notes about every country in the world. See **Appendix D** to find the link, scroll down to Spain and get the government's view of the country. It makes interesting reading. The State Department of the US also issues travel warnings concerning areas of the world where travelers may encounter problems because of unrest or other disturbances. The area in Spain through which the Camino runs at times has problems with local factions. Check the Travel Warnings page before you go to make sure there are no warnings.

In addition to web sites about the Camino, there are groups with others of a like mind. Sites of this kind come and go on the internet. They can be found by doing an internet search. You can join these sites and receive emails about commonly asked questions and the answers. There is also a wealth of information on each site. These types of sites are the most current as to what is happening on the Camino at the time you will be going. See **Appendix D** for a list of links to current sites.

There are many resources available and there are no limits as to what can be found. Each person will find their own body of knowledge to take with them. I first read Shirley MacLaine's book five years before making the trip. During the intervening time, I spent many hours on the internet just reading about associated topics. I read accounts of others on their web pages. With each new piece of information, I became more intrigued. The Camino was calling and I knew I had to go. Even after completing my journey, I still keep up with information about the Camino.

A few trips to the library and a few hours on the internet learning about Spain will be well worth it. You will be much more comfortable when you encounter an unusual Spanish custom or find yourself in an experience entirely new for you.

Emotional Expectations and Preparation

If you do not live in Spain, you will be entering a different culture. A phenomenon known as Culture Shock can occur and can send emotions reeling and upset even the most seasoned traveler. If you are not aware of Culture Shock, then you might attribute problems to other causes. If you have never traveled outside your home country, this is very likely to occur. Even the well traveled will experience it when going into a new environment. It is well worth it to be aware of what could happen and what to do to rectify it.

Culture shock can be defined as the emotional reaction that occurs when a person is subjected to a new environment, with different social customs, norms, foods, physical environment and forms of communication. Not all of these differences must be present for Culture Shock to occur. This can be explained by using an example one might encounter anywhere.

If a hearing person is suddenly put on the campus of a deaf school, where all communication is by sign language, the hearing person will suffer some level of culture shock when communication is attempted and not comprehended. An attempted communication could be initiated by either side. The hearing impaired, upon seeing a new person may attempt to sign a greeting to start a conversation. This greeting would not be understood, and the hearing person would not be able to respond according to the accepted norms. The hearing impaired person might then interpret the newcomer as distant, unfriendly, even hostile, or unintelligent because even basic interactions were not reciprocated in the accepted manner. This may result in negative feelings. The hearing impaired person may be more likely to understand the situation of a newcomer in the environment, but is also likely to feel resentment that the newcomer has not taken the time to understand the environment he has entered and learned a few signs in order to be able to communicate basic needs. If the hearing person first attempted communication by speaking, the spoken words would not even be perceived by the intended recipient. If the recipient is looking in another direction, the communication would not even be noticed. Thus the newcomer might interpret the intended recipient as being unconcerned and self-absorbed. After the newcomer has not been able to communicate and have basic needs met for a period of time, this person would probably begin to withdraw from contact and conclude that the campus was inhabited with strange individuals who did not know how to treat people. The newcomer would long to leave this place and go back where he came from. He would conclude that the people here were inferior to his own people and he would form negative impressions about his current environment. The newcomer is suffering from ethnocentrism and culture shock. There are ways to avoid these kinds of misunderstandings.

The phenomenon of Culture Shock occurs in a predictable sequence of four stages. These stages may overlap, but all of them will be felt to some degree. Depending on the length of time spent in a different environment and the ability or inability to find familiar customs to cling to, the length of time spent in each stage will vary from individual to individual. The important thing is to be aware of what is happening as it is happening to you. Denial can make things worse.

The first stage is sometimes called the "honeymoon" because everything seems wonderful. The new country is perceived as exciting and invigorating. Differences are seen as quaint and there are no negative perceptions. There is a feeling of euphoria and it seems as if everything is going to be marvelous. There are no problems at this stage.

The second stage, sometimes called "shock," usually starts emerging when a difficult situation presents itself. This situation could be any number of things. It could be the necessity to communicate something and not know how to do it. It could be the desire for a certain unavailable item. It could be homesickness. It could be having a problem of any kind that needs to be solved and not being able to solve it in the normal manner. It could be illness from food or an inability to obtain usual medications. It could be from failure to communicate or to respond to communication. Whatever the form of the external situation, the internal perceptions and emotions begin to change and certain symptoms will emerge. It is not necessary for all symptoms to occur to be in Culture Shock. If even two or three of the following occur, you are experiencing it:

- Feelings of helplessness
- Irritability, impatience, anger
- Stress
- Extreme homesickness
- Excessive sleep or sleeplessness
- Depression
- Overreaction to minor events
- Crying for no reason
- Hypersensitivity to illness – upset stomach, headaches
- Boredom
- Sadness
- Feelings of incompetence
- Feelings of superiority to local culture, extreme loyalty to native country
- Confusion
- Disorientation
- Overeating or lack of appetite, excessive alcohol use

There were a few times when I asked myself, "Why am I doing this?!?" It was usually during an uphill climb when I was taking baby steps to conserve energy to make it to the top. I was not comfortable and I wondered why I was putting myself through the physical torture. It would be much easier to fly into Santiago and take a taxi to the Cathedral. There was a point after a couple weeks of walking when part of me did not think I could make the entire 500 miles. But another small part of me whispered, "Yes, you can. That is why you are here. Keep going."

The length of time in the second stage will vary from individual to individual depending on how well the person recognizes the symptoms and does something about them. All pilgrims who I spoke to for any length of time expressed one or two symptoms and questioned their reasons for being in a particular situation. But all of the pilgrims kept going. Luckily, there are things you can do to lessen the symptoms and go to the third stage, aptly named "negotiation" or "acculturation." This is the stage when you realize the problem and start to do something about it. Here is a list of pro-active things you can do to go from "shock" to "negotiation" or "acculturation:"

✓ One of the things most often recommended to combat Culture Shock is exercise! Fortunately, you will be getting a lot of exercise whether you are walking or cycling. So keep going. Do not let the symptoms get you down. Persevere in your plan for walking a certain distance each day.

✓ Improve your Spanish skills. Get out the phrasebook and learn a new phrase each day. Pick something useful and you can apply it immediately. The language will become more familiar and be less intimidating. Spaniards are appreciative of travelers who try to speak Spanish. They will help you with the words and the pronunciation.

✓ If you can, find other pilgrims who speak your language or are from your country. You will discover that they are feeling the same way or have been through those emotions. Give each other support, but do not wallow in expressing negative opinions about anything. Your aim is to keep everything positive and keep going.

✓ Make sure you are eating well. If you have only been eating fruit because you can carry it easily or if you have been skipping meals to save money, it is time to splurge and seek out a Pilgrim's Menu for a well-rounded, nutritious meal. Buy some food to prepare in an albergue and strike up a conversation with other pilgrims. Many times I saw a sharing of food at the evening meal that resulted in everyone having a feast not feasible for one pilgrim to prepare. This can have the added benefit of camaraderie and good conversation.

✓ Realize what you are experiencing and intellectually tell yourself that you are in the process of transitioning in order to be able to understand and function in this culture.

✓ Think about what you are accomplishing. Focus on things you can do rather than what is causing you problems. Get out your map. See how far you have traveled. You are fulfilling goals every day.

✓ If the trip seems overwhelming, restate your goals so they are smaller and more quickly obtainable. Take one day at a time and experience it fully for its positive aspects. Evaluate your progress so far. You got yourself on the Camino. It is a lot further than many ever go.

✓ If you are traveling with people who seem to be suffering from culture shock worse than you are, try to distance yourself from them emotionally and do not be caught up in negative opinions and discussions that put-down host people, customs, norms or ideas. If you find yourself in a situation you can not get out of, try to be positive.

✓ Do a reality check. Think about the expectations you had when you began the trip. How close were they to reality? Modify your expectations to fit with the current reality. If there is something you wanted to do, but now find you cannot, let it go. It is something you do not need in your life. Along the trail, I was looking forward to seeing the famous chickens in Santo Domingo de la Calzada. On the day we arrived there, my husband pulled a muscle in his leg and I spent the afternoon locating a pharmacy that carried elastic bandages. Many pharmacies were sold out of these bandages, and I had to visit several before I finally located something helpful. When I returned, the church was closed and the chickens were in bed for the night. Oh well. My husband needed me and I was grateful to be able to help him. A reality check reduced my disappointment.

✓ Realize what you can control and what you can not control. Do something about the things you can control and let go of the things that you cannot. If it is driving you crazy to sleep with 20 other people every night, splurge and stay in a private room for a few days. You may find you miss having the energy of the other pilgrims close by.

✓ Remember that knowledge is power. Think back to all the research you did before the journey and review the information and how it might be applied to your current situation. You may find you know more than you think you do.

✓ Maintain your sense of humor. Smile a lot. Laugh frequently. See the humor in whatever situation you find yourself. Keep everything in perspective. You chose to go on this journey. Think back to the reasons you had for doing it.

✓ Acknowledge that you are suffering from one or more of the symptoms of Culture Shock and actively seek out something to combat it. Some things are effective for some people; others will do completely different things. Know what works for you and do it. Above all, be patient with yourself. You will make it.

These suggestions will take you through the acculturation stage. It won't happen all at once. You will waver on certain points and argue with yourself. But one morning you will wake up and discover no negative symptoms from the previous day. When that happens for a few days in a row, you will know you have progressed to the fourth state of "acceptance" or "stability." In this stage your emotions calm down. The people of the region again seem likable, rational, intelligent and friendly. They may seem to have idiosyncrasies, but those idiosyncrasies are charming. Your confidence, energy and enthusiasm returns and you wonder why you ever had a problem in the first place. Your mood swings are gone and you find the forced smiles made while you were in shock, are now natural and spontaneous. You feel great and can conquer the world or at least this part of it by getting to Santiago.

I also want to mention a fifth stage: reverse culture shock. This will occur when you return to your native country. After going through all the changes in perception that occurred while you are on the Camino, you come to think of Spain as a wonderful country and the Spanish people as having some different ideas worthy of merit. When you return home, these differences will again be apparent. However, now you will be thinking you have encountered better ways of doing things. You want to tell everyone about your experience and all these wonderful new things you have incorporated into your life. Your friends continued their lives while you were gone and are content with the status quo. They do not want to hear about why their tried-and-true ways are inferior to the new things you have experienced. For the sake of your friendships, temper your enthusiasm when returning home. You may not believe that this will happen, but trust me, it will. I have seen my friends go into an altered state and their eyes glaze over as I rant on about the Spanish countryside beauty, superiority, spirituality, and etc., etc., etc……. I have since learned to wait until they inquire about my experiences and give them small doses of information. If they continue to ask, I continue to talk. Otherwise I steer the conversation to what they did during the time I was gone. I want to keep my friends.

Spiritual Expectations and Preparation

So what exactly is a pilgrimage? In its broadest sense, it is defined as a sacred journey. By that definition, a pilgrimage can take place in the mind alone. One can meditate, pray, or otherwise commune with a higher power and gain peace, contentment or even enlightenment. However, the usual meaning involves physically going someplace else. It is a journey not only of the mind, but of the body, the spirit, the emotions and the soul all contributing to the effort.

There are a few characteristics of all pilgrimages, no matter the religion or reason for going.

- A pilgrimage involves physically going to another place. This allows a pilgrim to get away from problems and distractions in life and concentrate on the purpose for going. It means adapting to new surroundings which may include a different country, culture and language.

- A pilgrimage involves something spiritual or religious. The focus is on the soul, atma, afterlife, enlightenment or some aspect of spirituality.

- A pilgrimage usually involves some sort of sacrifice. A pilgrim gives up some of the amenities of modern life in order to experience spiritual growth.

- A pilgrimage usually involves some sort of introspection. A pilgrim may meditate, review their life path, or contemplate their place in the universe. It is a time for getting away from the usual, the routine, and experiencing something new and different.

- A pilgrimage is usually done alone. A pilgrim may physically have friends and others along on the journey, but the real pilgrimage takes place in the very core of the individual. Each day is experienced, absorbed and transformed into the new individual that will emerge at the end of the journey.

- A pilgrimage usually involves a span of time. They are not undertaken over a weekend, a week or even a month. The time leading up to the actual journey is also part of the pilgrimage because it involves the mental thought needed to organize all the physical, mental, spiritual, emotional and logistical things that must come together in order to undertake the journey.

- A pilgrimage involves a holy site of some sort. This can be a place where a saint or holy person lived or had a major transformation (Bodh Gaya, place of Buddha's enlightenment, Garden of Gesemini) or a place where a relic is housed (Black Stone at Mecca, bones of various saints at churches worldwide, including Santiago) or a place where a vision has been seen (Lourdes).

All major religions have pilgrimages. Followers of Islam go to Mecca for the Hajj. Hindus go to the River Ganges. Buddhism has the Bodhgaya. Silhism practices Amritsar. Judaism, Islam and Christianity share a sacred site in the city of Jerusalem. Catholicism has specific places, such as Lourdes and Santiago. Antiquity had pilgrimages to such places as Thebes, Delphi, Temple of Diana or Dodona, many times to seek the advice of an oracle. Sometimes the physical place is sacred to more than one religion.

The word "Pilgrimage" is even used in a secular meaning, as a visitor to Graceland, Elvis Presley's home will attest. There are also "tourist Meccas," which are places that draw people in. The Mausoleums of Lenin in Moscow and Mao Zedong in Beijing are pilgrimage sites for thousands who follow their teachings. The Paris grave of rock star Jim Morrison, draws a large following every year.

The ubiquity of the practice lends credibility to the effort. Let's review a few of these practices to see the similarities and differences.

Islam

The Islamic pilgrimage to Mecca can be traced back 4000 years to a time when it was not just Muslims who completed the journey. Anyone who felt the spiritual longing could travel and go through the rituals. The pilgrimage started because of an incident with Abraham, his wife Hajra and his infant son Ismael. Abraham was away one day when Ismael became thirsty. Hajra tried to find water and had to run seven times, searching for water. Water was finally found when, either, Ismael stamped his foot or an angel's wing touched the ground and water was produced. The running and the finding of water is the basis for part of the ritual today.

The Hajj, or pilgrimage, took on its modern day approach when Muhammad completed the pilgrimage and rituals in the year 632 CE. It is at this point the Hajj became one of the five pillars of Islam and something all Muslims must do at least once in their lives if they have the means to do it. The rituals are very specific and detailed. All pilgrims travel to Mecca at the same time every year and perform the rituals together. There is strict regulation of clothing, food and behavior while on the pilgrimage. Some of the rules have been altered because of the large crowds that gather (1,613,000 in 2009). For example, it is now acceptable for pilgrims to point to the Black Stone in the Sacred Mosque rather than kissing it. With that minor change, thousands of pilgrims can all partake in the ritual simultaneously.

The Hajj involves running between two sites, simulating Hajra's search for water, traveling to Mina, a neighboring city, throwing stones at a symbolic devil and sacrificing an animal. All these rituals have taken on a modern affectation to accommodate the growing crowds and to take advantage of modern conveniences. However the spiritual content remains the same.

Hinduism, Buddhism and Jainism

The Ganges River is held sacred by Hindus, Buddhists and Janists. The city of Varanasi (or Benares or Banaras) is where this is most exemplified and is one of four pilgrimage sites suggested by Gautama Buddha. The Janists believe it is the birthplace of one of their sacred forefathers.

In Varanasi the Ganges is lined with ghats, buildings with steps down into the river. Each ghat is unique in what is offers the pilgrim. Some are for bathing only. Some are for cremation. One boasts that it is the place where Buddha received enlightenment. Others have connections with various Hindu gods, such as Lord Shiva and Lord Brahma. Lord Shiva is said to have founded the city 5000 years ago.

The ritual bathing in the Ganges will wash away all sins. If a person should die while on the pilgrimage in Varansi, his/her soul is released from the cycle of reincarnation.

Christianity

The pilgrimage possibilities are many and varied. There are sites worldwide that draw pilgrims in but they are concentrated in Europe and the Americas. The most famous would be the Holy Lands, with several sites, some shared with followers of Islam and Judaism. One of the oldest pilgrimages is to Santiago de Compostala, the tomb of St. James.

Each individual site has traditions, customs and rituals that allow the pilgrim to complete the tasks and gain favor. There are no set times for undertaking a pilgrimage. Whenever it is convenient or whenever the call is heard, is fine for starting.

Why go?

Throughout the ages the reasons for going on a pilgrimage have changed little. In medieval times many people were told they must go on a pilgrimage in penance for some sin. Depending on the severity of the sin, they were even told they must complete the pilgrimage barefoot or even naked. However, most went willingly of their own accord in order to satisfy some personal longing.

Before modern communication with radio, television and now live images over the internet, pilgrims often experienced a need to go places where certain events took place or to touch relics. This brought about a deepening of faith and an internal satisfaction that these places and things were real.

One of the main reasons given for going on a pilgrimage is to have a better relationship, or get closer to God. Time away from the usual routines of daily life allow a person to focus on sacred and divine subjects. Thoughts and beliefs can become clearer. God is better defined and understood.

Some feel the need to be relieved of the guilt of sin. Pilgrimages offer a unique experience and all seem to have forgiveness as part of the rituals. Pilgrims can turn negative actions into hope for the future.

Certain destinations offer specific healing of the body. Many with afflictions will travel to a holy site to be cured. There are many such sites throughout the world. Belief is a strong healing power. Pilgrims can connect to a particular healing saint or deity and it can have a positive effect on the soul as well as the body.

Sometimes a question is in the mind of the pilgrim that must be answered. A difficult decision must be made and divine guidance is sought. Being away from the routine can clear the mind and a connection with God can help solve ethical or moral dilemmas.

Some embark on a pilgrimage without any specific purpose other than personal transformation. The chance to travel, meet new people, meditate on one's life or think about the future can have a transformative effect on outlook and behavior.

Who goes on a pilgrimage?

In early times, the wealthy comprised most of the crowd going to pilgrimage sites. Although some commoners did make the journey, it was usually because of some personal circumstances or a mandate from the church. One of the earliest records of an organized pilgrimage is Chaucer's *The Canterbury Tales*. Although the motives of the pilgrims are not given, a wide spectrum of society is represented in the short 50 mile journey from London to the cathedral at Canterbury which houses the remains of Thomas Becket.

In Medieval times a pilgrimage may have been the only way people could travel. Going away from home was often dangerous and a pilgrim risked being robbed or even killed. For this reason, people often went in groups. Pilgrims from England and mainland Europe en route to Jerusalem would gather at a port in France and book passage across the Mediterranean. Pilgrims walking across Europe to Santiago de Compostela found their paths converging as they neared the site.

Today pilgrimages can be undertaken by almost anyone who has the desire and will.

Followers of non-Christian religions are often more adamant about making a pilgrimage. Muslims must try to find a way to Mecca at least once in their lives. Hindus flock to the Ganges to fulfill their religious beliefs. Many Christians, especially non-Catholics are not aware of the concept of a pilgrimage and only a small percentage have experienced one.

Your Pilgrimage

So now let's get personal. Something has sparked an interest in a pilgrimage and you picked up this book to get some more information. You've read through the sections on physical, mental and emotional expectations and preparation and they look doable. You can get physically ready, study up on Spanish culture and be aware of the Culture Shock symptoms and know how to combat them. Now let's examine your spiritual motives.

Think about the characteristics of a pilgrimage in this chapter. Are you willing to put up with all the different things that a pilgrimage will entail?

What is your reason for going on a pilgrimage? Examine the list given and be honest about why you want to go. Several forces could be involved.

What do you hope to accomplish? This is a tough one, but if you can be honest about your response, the greater the chance it will be fulfilled. Set a few reasonable spiritual goals. These will keep you going when times be come difficult and you become road-weary.

When I walked the Camino, I had no specific spiritual goals. I wanted to experience the journey and see what would happen. I had no overwhelming transformation. Changes were set in motion and I am still living the impact of my journey. I often have flashbacks to what seemed like an insignificant event. Obviously, they were not insignificant and I continue to marvel at the memories, both waking and sleeping, that influence me.

Set reasonable spiritual goals for yourself. You may want to experience full "enlightenment," but it probably won't happen while you are walking. The true pilgrimage started on the day when your interest was piqued. It will continue for the rest of your life.

Every pilgrim's journey is unique. As with most things in life, pilgrims probably end up learning what they need and not necessarily what they want. This is not always easy for the individual pilgrim to see.

I have read accounts of some pilgrims that were deeply moving and these pilgrims had profound spiritual transformations. Other pilgrims have experienced realizations that allowed them to live their lives more fully.   Still others reveled in the energy of the Camino and used the time to contemplate and meditate.

Preparation for your spiritual journey will be a very personal thing. You must do whatever your chosen belief system requires of you. Pray, meditate, cleanse your body and soul, repeat mantras, use prayer beads. Do what comforts you.

You may not realize what the Camino has given you until much later. While on the Camino, even the most spiritual person is so caught up in the process that there is little time for reflection of the results of that process. The best preparation may simply be an open mind.

Tip #3 Takeaways

❖ Expectations can set the tone for the entire experience.

❖ Make sure you are physically fit for the amount of the Camino you will be covering.

❖ Some knowledge of Spain and a few Spanish phrases will go a long way to make you feel comfortable in a foreign country.

❖ Understand Culture Shock and realize that you will experience it. Know how to combat the symptoms.

❖ Be realistic about what you want to accomplish spiritually. The experience will influence you the rest of your life.

Tip # 4

Know How to Get There,
Get Around
and
Get Back

Adventure is worthwhile.
-Amelia Earhart

If you don't know where you are going, you'll end up someplace else.
Yogi Berra

Nothing is worse than being lost in a foreign country. If you are familiar with how things are done there, then the situation becomes tolerable, maybe even fun.

Tip #4 – Know How to Get There, Get Around, and Get Back

Different Routes to Santiago

It is a surprise to most people that there is not just one, but several "Caminos." The most famous and the most traveled is the French Way or Camino Francés, which traditionally begins in St. Jean Pied-de-Port in southern France. There is also the Camino de la Plata, Camino Primitivo, Camino del Norte, Camino Portugués, Camino Ria de Arousa, Camino Inglés, Camino de Finisterre, Camino Valenciano and Camino Lucense. See **Appendix D** for a link to view all European routes to Santiago. When you think about it, more than one route makes sense. During the Middle Ages, when pilgrims began their journey, they stepped out of their homes and started walking. They started from places all over Europe and beyond, and as they approached Compostela, their routes converged. Most pilgrims came through Europe and one of the easier passageways across the Pyrenees goes through St. Jean Pied-de-Port. However, saying it is easier, is not saying it is easy.

The different routes offer different advantages and disadvantages to the pilgrim. My husband and I chose the French Way and we also chose to start at St. Jean Pied-de-Port. We did this for several reasons. We wanted to follow the traditional path because we thought there would be more history along this path. Also, because of the popularity, there would be more places to stay and more consideration given to pilgrims. And, quite truthfully, we did not realize so many other paths were available.

As we neared Santiago, we did meet pilgrims who had come on alternate paths. A curious fact emerged. Many times, a pilgrim who came on a different path was doing so only after having walked the traditional Camino Frances at some time in the past. The other routes were secondary adventures chosen after the traditional path.

One of the first decisions you will have to make is to choose the route. Then determine a distance you will have time to cover. Once the route is chosen, choose an appropriate starting point along the route. Once the starting point is chosen, select the largest city near your starting point to fly into the country. It may be the same city where you have chosen to begin your walk or it may be another. Many people from outside Europe fly into Madrid and take a train to the starting point from which they will actually begin to walk. The Spanish train and bus systems are both modern and comfortable for long or short distance travel.

Time Differences and Jet Lag

To make these plans you can book a flight online or talk to your favorite travel agent. Several online travel sites are listed in **Appendix D**. Because of jet lag and the rigors of travel, I recommend staying at least one, possibly two nights in a regular hotel before starting the Camino. It is also a good ideal to book a one or two night stay at the same hotel before departing after your walk is complete. Let me explain.

Staying in the same hotel for a few nights at the beginning and end of your journey will serve more than one purpose. First, it will allow your body to adapt a bit to the change in time when you arrive. When you are leaving, it will give you a couple days of rest before you return to your normal life. If you are someone who is not affected by jet lag or if you know some of the tricks for avoiding it, then you can use the extra day to explore the city where your adventure began. You can also use this time to arrange something for your extra luggage.

If you have carefully prepared your backpack for walking the Camino, then you do not have extra clothes for travel and for activities before and after the trek. Most people, however, do take extras for other activities not related to the Camino. There are a few things you can do with the additional luggage.

What to do with Extra Luggage

You will have to put your backpack in checked luggage to get it to Spain. The typical backpack has many straps and pockets vulnerable to being broken or torn. A simple solution is to purchase a plain duffle bag big enough to hold the backpack and the few extra things that you want on the trip. This will protect your backpack and will allow you to take some spare things. When you arrive in country, you can extract the backpack and be ready to go, but what do you do with the extra things while you are walking?

One solution is to ask your hotel to hold it for you. Most European hotels have a service they call "luggage storage." Depending on the hotel, they will hold it for a few hours or days, or another specified time frame. Some hotels are friendlier than others in what they will do for you. If you stay with them upon arriving, and can assure them of reservations upon the termination of your trek, they will be more likely to accommodate you. Thus, the money spent for a nice room at the beginning and end of your journey can offset some other costs if the hotel is agreeable about holding your extra luggage. Try to keep the extra amount as small as possible, because space is at a premium in all European cities, and the space your duffle takes up is a cost to the hotel, especially if they do the same for many pilgrims.

We flew into Bilbao and stayed at a hotel which is part of an American chain. On the internet, the literature listed luggage storage service, but when we first inquired, the desk clerk said they would only hold luggage for a few hours. I explained that we were going to walk the Camino and would be gone for about two months and needed a place to store our extra items. The desk clerk was intrigued with two Americans who not only knew about the Camino, but were actually going to walk it. We had a lively conversation about the Camino. The clerk said that he had not walked it yet, but was waiting until his young son would be old enough to accompany him. I reminded him of our return reservations and how help from him would ease our situation. He asked how many bags we wanted to leave. We told him it would be just one. I am sure he was thinking about where he would put it. He verified our future reservations and said he would talk with the hotel manager about the situation. We were able to leave one bag containing all our extras with the hotel while we were on our journey.

Both my husband and I had purchased duffel bags for our backpacks and extra things. When we removed the backpacks, we were able to fold up one duffle and put it in the other along with all the extra clothes we had both brought. I also left my purse, minus any money and identification documents. We made sure there was an identification tag on the outside of the duffle and one inside as well. The morning we checked out to take the bus to France, we felt we had left our belongings in secure hands. Actually, I am not sure if our extra duffle was in fact stored at the hotel or if the desk clerk took it home to keep it for us. It does not matter. When we returned, our duffle was waiting for us, just as we had left it. I also made sure to bring the clerk a small gift of a coffee mug from Santiago. He was very appreciative.

Sending Things Ahead

If the hotel you chose is not obliging or if you choose not to leave your extra luggage at a hotel, there is another option available. It is the Spanish postal system. General delivery is available in the main post office of all major cities. It is possible to send a package to yourself and then pick it up when you get there. Many pilgrims will box up their extra luggage and send it to Santiago. When they arrive there, they can then pick up their extras at the main post office near the Cathedral. If you want to use this option, be very particular about how you address the package. Your hotel may be able to find a box for you. If not, there are stores in some cities selling mailing cartons. Ask your hotel where you can find one. You may be able to put a label directly on your luggage and ship it that way.

General delivery is known as "Lista de Correos" in Spanish. It is also called "Poste Restante" in French and both are recognized by the Spanish post office. To send a package to General Delivery in Santiago, the label you put on the package should be in the following format:

Your Name
Lista de Correos
15780 Santiago de Compostela (A Corona)
Spain

Make sure you print your name legibly and exactly as it is on your country passport. You will use your country passport as identification when you are picking up the package. Both names must match exactly or you will have problems trying to get your things. "Lista de Correos" identifies this bundle as going into the general delivery bin. The next line identifies the postal code for Santiago as 15780 and also lists the name of the city. The county is in parenthesis. This is to avoid any confusion. And on last line, the country is listed.

Ask at the post office where you mail your package as to how long it will take to get there. They will keep a package for 30 days once it has reached its destination, although I suspect that they may hold it longer or not, depending on the number of pilgrims using the service at any one time. To ensure your package does not get posted back to your origination point, you might put the return address as Santiago also. As of this writing, there is no charge for using the general delivery service.

When you arrive in Santiago and want to claim your package, make sure you have your identification with you. Go to the main post office.

As many pilgrims use this service, there are times when there is a large influx of packages for the postal personnel to handle. There is little organization in how they store the packages, so if you can make yours distinct, it may be easier for a clerk to find. Put stickers on the package, or draw a unique design on one side - anything to make your package stand out. Take a picture of it with your digital camera before you mail it and show the picture to the clerk when you are claiming it. Make sure your name is in large easy-to-read letters. And remember that Spanish bureaucracy is alive and well. It may take quite a bit of time to find your bundle. Be patient and helpful.

The astute reader will realize that this service could be used for sending supplies along the road as well as to the final destination. If you simply cannot use any other brand of shampoo than the one you usually use and it is not available in Europe, you can send a bottle to particular cities and not have to carry them the entire way. This may take some advance planning and patience, as delivery times may vary from city to city. It is also possible to send supplies directly from your home country. Be sure to factor in additional time for arrival in the desired city. For some common city postal codes in both France and Spain, this site can help: http://www.csj.org.uk/faqs.htm#intouch. If the city you want is not listed, do a Google search for "desired city country postal code."

Buses, Trains and Taxis

Public transportation in Europe is excellent. There are modern buses, trains and airplanes to take you to your desired starting point. Once you have made arrangements for your extra luggage, it is then time to arrange to get to your starting point for walking. Your hotel or guidebook can lead you to the appropriate bus or train station to get you where you want to go. It is usually not necessary to purchase your ticket in advance, but you can do this if you desire. You will probably have to go to the appropriate station to find the schedule to the city you have chosen. When you are checking the schedule, go ahead and purchase your ticket.

When you arrive at the city you have chosen, find the albergue and get your documents as explained in **Tip #5**. Hopefully you will not have complications along the way. We had a few. Getting to Saint Jean Pied-de-Port from Bilbao involves taking a bus to the French city of Bayonne and then a train to Saint Jean Pied-de-Port. We purchased a ticket for the first bus out of Bilbao at 6:00AM. We had the seats in the front and thoroughly enjoyed the scenery as we sped along the coast to Bayonne. The trip took about four hours and we were delighted to find ourselves in the city in the early part of the day. I had a map of the city from a travel book so it was easy to find our way the six or so blocks from the bus station to the train station. However, upon arriving at the train station, we found it to be eerily deserted. A quick look at the large schedule posted in the main room confirmed that there would be a train to Saint Jean Pied-de-Port in a couple of hours. The windows for purchasing tickets were, however, closed. I wondered about this mystery, but thought maybe there were few trains running that day and the windows would open closer to the time of departure. But a look at the schedule revealed departure times within the next half hour. I was confused, but not yet panicked.

There were a few other perplexed people walking around, so I knew something was amiss. I also knew that the only public transportation into Saint Jean Pied-de-Port is the train, so there might possibly be other pilgrims who desired to go there. Several of the perplexed looking people did, indeed, look like pilgrims, as they had the requisite backpacks. I overheard Spanish being spoken and picked up the word "huelga," meaning "strike." I listened further to hear a discussion about the French train workers who were on strike. There would be no passage today. We struck up a conversation with a woman who looked like, and was indeed, a pilgrim. She spoke no English, but she did speak

Spanish and French, so she was able to translate the notices posted in the train station. There was indeed a strike. What to do now?

I consulted my map. The tourist office was located next to the bus station where we had just arrived. We decided to go there to see if we could possibly find other transportation. This turned out to be a wise move. Neither my husband nor I speak any French, so we had to find someone who spoke either English or Spanish to help us out. The workers at the tourist office spoke both, so we were able to communicate our problem. They were not aware of the situation. We explained that we were pilgrims and that we were trying to get to Saint Jean Pied-de-Port to start our journey. The worker at the tourist office made a few quick phone calls and verified the strike. She was very aware that this was the only type of transport available. As we were talking with her, others who had been in the train station started arriving and expressing the same concern. Altogether, there were ten prospective pilgrims trying to get to Saint Jean Pied-de-Port.

At this point, several of the tourist office personnel were involved, and many phone calls were being placed. We were told to go back to the train station and they would arrange for a bus to take us. We did as we were told and at the time the train would have normally left, a bus pulled up in the parking lot of the train station. Word spread among the waiting pilgrims that this would be our transport. The driver was French and spoke no other language. He announced something in the train station. The French-Spanish speaking pilgrim who we had met earlier translated and we all headed for the bus. We attempted to pay the driver as we boarded, but he would not accept any money. The Bayonne tourist office had arranged for the bus to take the pilgrims to their destination free of charge. We were flabbergasted. In hindsight, it was the first of many considerations given to us as pilgrims.

Fast forward on to Santiago. We have completed our journey, spent a few days marveling at the wonders of the city and have bought some keepsakes to take back home. Our extra luggage is in Bilbao, but our lockers at the Santiago albergue are bursting at the seams with newly-acquired purchases. Not everything will fit in our backpack. We have decided to take the train back to Bilbao and are eagerly anticipating a leisurely journey, but do not want to be burdened with a multitude of plastic bags to transport our purchases. That problem was easily and economically solved with the additional purchase of a medium-sized zippered carrier, which was able to accommodate all our purchases and made transporting them easy. These carriers can be purchased in the market near the Cathedral for about seven euros.

At this point, we were no longer using our walking sticks, and we knew they would be cumbersome on a train, bus or plane, but we wanted to keep them as we both had grown quite attached. We solved that problem by packaging them in paper and cardboard so they could be easily carried and would be accepted as checked baggage when we made our final trip back to the states. We asked at the albergue if we could have the used newspaper the attendant read each morning. He was happy to oblige and we wrapped both staffs in a generous layer of Spanish news. We were able to find a cardboard box which we dismantled into a flat piece of cardboard, then wrapped the staffs in it to create a carton of sorts. Lots of plastic wrapping tape provided the final layer to protect our staffs all the way back to our home. There was no problem carrying this on the train or, subsequently on the plane. Unwrapped staffs are not allowed on planes these days, so if you want to bring back your staff, wrap it well.

Passenger train service in the United States consists of a few routes between selected cities and can be expensive, usually slow and not of much use. Neither my husband nor I had ridden in a train in the US or a European train, so there were a few things to learn as we went along. When we purchased our tickets from Santiago to Bilbao at the Pilgrim's Office (See **Tip #5** for that information), the clerk told us we would change seats in one of the cities. I thought that was rather strange and asked if we could have the same seat for the entire distance. She said it was not possible, and I took it to mean that someone else had already booked the seat for part of the trip. That was not the case. But I digress. Let me explain our new-found knowledge the same way it unfolded for us.

We took a taxi to the Santiago train station with tickets in hand. As we are used to plane travel, we arrived a little early not knowing what the check-in procedure would be. There is no check-in procedure. You have a ticket which indicates a particular car on the train and a particular seat on that car. The car numbers are clearly marked next to the entrance doors. I did not know what we would do with our luggage and there was no one to ask, as the ticket windows were closed. I experienced a momentarily frightening déjà vu back to Bayonne, until I noticed and followed an inconspicuous "Information" sign posted over a door. It led into a small office with one person behind a desk. He did not seem busy, so I approached and started to talk. I told him it was my first train ride and I was wondering what to do with the luggage. He sized me up as a novice in both train travel and explaining the situation in Spanish and patiently explained that there was space at both ends of every car for passengers to personally place their luggage. Simply stash it there when we got on and pick it up as we got off. Simple. The reality was exactly as he had described. There is a generous space at each end of the car for any luggage. Passengers were courteous and put the luggage in an orderly fashion and there was enough room for everything.

About 10 minutes before the train was scheduled to leave, the conductor allowed us to board the train, where we discovered the luggage space, found a spot for ours and then proceeded to our seats. The seat numbers we had were not side by side, but rather back to back. My husband's seat was facing backwards and there was another gentleman from the states who had the seat facing him, so that their knees were touching. My seat was facing forward with my back to my husband.   The train was not full and as we pulled out of the station I saw that there was no one sitting in the seat next to my husband, so I quickly moved.   I thought this arrangement of some passengers riding backwards to be unusual, but as I glanced around the car, several of the seats were in this configuration. We struck up a conversation with the gentleman who was sharing knee space with my husband. It was his first train trip also and he was feeling a bit uncomfortable in such close proximity. He suggested we switch seats to both be more comfortable. We did so.

A few minutes into the ride and the conductor came around to check our tickets. He noticed the seat exchange, and asked if everyone was content with the arrangement.   We said we were, so he did not do anything about sitting in the wrong seats.

The route of the train retraced our pilgrim's route going backward through the major cities.   When we were walking, we had observed trains on several occasions. I was sure we were being observed by pilgrims still on the trail. The train stopped in all the large cities and some of the smaller ones as well. Some passengers got off and new ones got on. At one stop, after the train pulled into the station, we heard loud noises of metal on metal. Train cars were being moved. The engine was uncoupled from the front of the train, and by using a side track, was put on the other end of the train. We were now going in the opposite direction. Then several people in the car stood up, took a firm hold on the handle of the back of the seat and moved it so they could sit down facing forward and still be in the same seat. My jaw dropped as I witnessed this transformation.   My husband and I looked at each other and promptly got up to see if our seat also possessed these amazing properties. It did.

An explanation is in order here for those of you who are as ignorant as I was concerning the construction of train seats.   Train cars have a connection at both ends which allow them to be connected with another car and engine. Consequently, a train car can travel in either direction. As most passengers prefer to face forward when in a moving vehicle, the seats have been constructed so the back of the seat is on a swivel allowing it to be on either the "front" or "back" of a seat. Thus, if a train pulls into a station one way and must go out on the same track in the opposite direction and the cars cannot be physically turned around, the engine can simply be connected to the other end of the train and it can pull out of the station and be on its way. Passengers can choose to reconfigure their seats to face forward, or they can leave the seats as they are. If some of the seats are changed and others not, it will result in the configuration we found upon first entering the train, with some facing forward and some facing back and some passengers sharing knee space. This change in direction happened at several stops during the day's journey, and we became expert in switching the seat to keep facing forward.

At one point, we pulled into the station and were told to get off the train. This is where the change in seat number was to take place. Actually, it was not just a seat change, but also a car change. The particular car we were in was headed for a different city, so we had to get on the car going to our destination. We gathered our things, including our luggage, and went to the station platform. It took about 20 minutes for the changes to take place and we watched in fascination as some cars were taken off and others added to the train. We found the car indicated by the number on our ticket and boarded to find our new seats. We now felt like veteran train travelers as we adjusted the seat back to face forward.

Our journey took most of the day. We had not brought anything to eat, and noticed that some people were getting up and returning with a sandwich to munch on. We decided to explore and found a dining car with a limited seating capacity, but with a snack bar with sandwiches, sodas and potato chips. The sandwiches were quite good and we were able to complete our journey without hunger pangs setting in.

Tip #4 Takeaways

❖ There are many routes to Santiago. The French Route is the most popular.

❖ Give yourself time to adjust to jet lag.

❖ You can send supplies and backpacks ahead.

❖ Trains and busses are ubiquitous and can help you get around.

Tip #5

Some Good Things to Know

It is not necessarily the person who knows, but the person who knows how to find out.
Herbert K. Vetter

The above quote is by my father, who always encouraged me to explore the world. He felt that no person could be an expert on everything, but one could find out anything. It is important to have curiosity and know how to satisfy it. In this chapter, I give to you many interesting and essential things that I found out.

Tip #5 – Some Good Things to Know

There are some miscellaneous things that just make life easier, especially when traveling in a foreign country. These are things about the Camino in particular and Spain in general that give peace of mind.

Albergues or Refugios?

Most of the sources of information we had when researching for this trip referred to "refugios" or refuges as places to stay along the Camino. When we got there, the word used most often was "albergue." In the area of southern France and northern Spain, the words are used interchangeably. As we got further away from France, "refugio" was not used and "albergue" was the word to look for on buildings and to use when asking for a place to stay.

Types of Albergues

Albergue is a Spanish word meaning shelter or hostel. It implies very basic accommodations. Along the Camino there are three types of albergues: those run by the Catholic Church, those run by local municipalities, and those run by private individuals. Each type offers different amenities and pricing.

The albergues run by the Church are the backbone of the Camino. They are the traditional stopping places and offer a glimpse into history as many of them are several hundred years old. They continue to be run by people associated with the Church, usually nuns or monks, who are part of an order. These albergues have the strictest rules and offer the least amenities. There is a bed. There may or may not be a pillow or blanket. The rooms are large and there are many beds close together. When these facilities are full, they feel crowded and cramped.

Many times the crowding seemed intentional. It is easier to maintain and clean up a facility if the location of the pilgrims is controllable. If there are three large rooms available, the assignments will start in one room and only overflow to another when the first is filled. Another system used in the larger Church run facilities is to separate pilgrims by sex and marital status. In León, single females were put in one large room, single males in another, and married couples in the third large room. The night we stayed there, more single males arrived than could be accommodated in their room and the overflow was put in with the married couples.

There was another system used in a monastery in Carrión de los Condes. The facility had many small rooms rather than a few large ones. Pilgrims were assigned to a room with others of the same sex. In our case, as a married couple, we were given a small room with three beds. We thought we might have a room to ourselves, but a short time later another gentleman arrived to occupy the third bed. We had heard about this practice which was a deterrent for any unseemly activities while staying there.

There may or may not be hot water in the Church run facilities. Or the hot water may run out early in the day. They are also strict about closing the facility at a specific hour and locking up. If you have registered, left your belongings on your bed, gone exploring and found something to occupy you past the closing hour, you will have to find another place to sleep. If you are not inside when the doors are locked, you are out of luck. This is not a problem for most pilgrims; just make sure you are aware of the curfew time. It can be as early as 9:00 PM.

There will also be a time in the morning by which you must leave. Usually, around 8:00 AM or 8:30 AM. Some places will wake you up. In Roncevalles, we were slumbering with about 150 of our new best friends, when, at precisely 6:00 AM, the church bells rang out, the lights came on, and the monks came through the room wishing everyone a good morning. The motivation was obvious and soon everyone was scurrying about to pack up and get on the road. Similar rituals were followed at several other places along the way.

The good news is they are cheap. The cost to stay in a church run albergue ranges from free to about five euros per bed. The cost varies from facility to facility. However, a bit more bad news is you can only stay for one night. An exception might be made if there is a physical problem. If you are hurt or sick, they will assist you and let you stay an additional night or two. No more. You must either get well and continue or quit and go home. In reality, in most cities, it is possible to move to a different kind of facility to rest, recuperate, or stay longer for personal reasons.

One step above the Church run facilities, in terms of comfort, are the albergues run by the local municipalities. These will have pillows and blankets, more available hot water, and the rooms will not be as crowded. Many municipally-run albergues are quite comfortable. Some may even have internet kiosks. They will cost between four and six euros per night per bed. This is for a one night stay only. However, the folks who run these are more lenient in allowing you additional time to stay with them for a non-health reason. If you request to stay another day, you must still pack up in the morning and remove all your belongings from the area. You will be allowed to leave your backpack in the albergue, usually behind the registration desk or some other inconspicuous place. You must leave the albergue but can return when it opens for the new pilgrims arriving that day. After all the new pilgrims have registered, including cyclists, if there is an available bed, you may have it. The risk is that the albergue could fill and then you must find other accommodations.

The most luxurious albergue, if those two words can be used together, are privately run. They offer all the amenities of the first two with more space around the beds. There are smaller rooms so occasionally, we had a space for just the two of us. Also, the beds are not always bunk beds. These facilities may fashion a row of small two people "rooms" featuring two beds on opposite sides of the walls and a small closet for personal items. These two-people arrangements still have some drawbacks, as these are not really rooms, but a portioned off area and any sound from the other areas still carries quite well. But the additional privacy for dressing and sleeping is welcome. There are still community showers to accommodate everyone.

All of the rooms in private albergues are small, from two to ten people in a room. The furniture and linens are still relatively new. Occasionally, there were sheets. These structures were often newly painted and had an air of modernity. Most private albergues had internet access and some even had a restaurant in the albergue or close by. There were various other amenities available at individual albergues. One even had a swimming pool. The cost of a private albergue was usually between five and eight euros per bed per night.

We ran across a few places that were a combination of albergue and hotel. They had part of the facility set up like an albergue with communal bathing facilities and various size sleeping rooms. But they also had regular hotel rooms with private baths, beds with complete linens, and towels and soap provided. These ranged from 20 to about 50 euros per night.

Of course, the medium to larger size cities and some of the vacation spots had hotels. Depending on the location, a room might cost upwards to several hundred euros a night. A regular tourist guide will have this information.

Every albergue is unique. It is part of the charm of the Camino. We ended up staying in all three types of facilities. When Shirley MacLaine wrote her popular book in the late 1990s, she talked about having to sleep in the open because of lack of space. This is no longer the case.

There is an abundance of possibilities for bedding down each night. A pilgrim sleeps under the stars only if that is the desired location.

So how does one go about finding all the available albergues? There are several resources. At the starting point of your journey, the facility that issues you your Pilgrim's Passport will probably have a list of the Church run facilities along the way. If it is not offered, ask for it. Your Camino guidebook, if you chose to purchase one, will also have a list of available facilities. This will contain most, but not all the Church run facilities and some of the municipal and private albergues. I did not see any book with a comprehensive list. But do not worry. The concept of advertising has sprung up on the Camino in a limited fashion, and new albergues are starting to "advertise" along the way. This is done in two different manners. Fliers are placed in albergues preceding the one being advertised. Check on the bulletin boards or around the registration desk for materials indicating upcoming albergues. You can then check your plans and if you are planning to stay in any particular city, you can seek out an advertised albergue. We found several very nice places from the advertisements.

As you near Santiago, albergues become more abundant and the advertising becomes more competitive. You will find fliers left under rocks in conspicuous places along the trail. If something appeals to you, take a flier and check out the place.

New albergues are constantly springing up along the Camino. Train your eye to be on the lookout for the word "albergue," as it may appear on the side of a building or on a sign in front of an establishment. It may be hand written or it may be professionally painted. The outside appearance is not always an indicator of the inside conveniences.

One process requested of pilgrims at a few albergues was to place shoes and staffs in a common area before proceeding to the sleeping rooms. The first time this happened, we were reluctant to leave our shoes for fear someone else might like them and decide to take them. The proprietor explained that it kept the sleeping quarters cleaner, so we obliged. A shelf was provided for storing the shoes, and we were always able to retrieve our own shoes the next morning. This also brings up the need for a second pair of some kind of footwear for wearing after hours.

We left our staffs in what looked like a large umbrella stand. We had previously each put our initials on them to avoid a mix-up with another. We had no problem finding our own staffs to proceed on the journey the next morning.

One final word on albergues: Not all albergues are open year round. A few are only open during the summer months when there is the most traffic. If you plan to travel in the early spring, late fall or winter, your choices will be more limited. The church run and municipal facilities will be open. It is the private ones that may not be. However, there is such an abundance of places, you will still find enough to accommodate your needs. It may just take a little more planning.

Pilgrim's Passport or Pilgrims Credentials

In order to stay at any accommodations for pilgrims, it is necessary to have the proper credentials. This means a "passport" issued by the organization that regulates the pilgrimage. This piece of paper identifies the person as someone who has registered to undertake the pilgrimage. It is only with a properly completed passport that a pilgrim can obtain a certificate of completion and be permanently registered on the rolls of the Cathedral in Santiago as a person who has fulfilled the necessary requirements of a pilgrim.

Several sources state you should bring a letter from your local parish concerning your desire to undertake the Camino. This is unnecessary. It is not necessary to be Catholic or even Christian to obtain a passport.

The only thing needed is to show up at one of the churches or offices issuing the passports and fill out the required forms. Where you plan to start your journey makes a difference as to where you can get your passport. The smaller cities and towns do not have them. You should start your journey in one of the larger towns along the route.

Once you choose your starting city, find out where both the Cathedral and tourist office are located. You can get this information from your guidebook, if you were able to purchase one in advance, or from a regular travel guide, if you were not. Check the internet to see if a map is available on line to locate these places for you. If that doesn't work, visit your local library and get the information explained below.

Go to the local Cathedral and ask about the office to get the credential. It will probably be at the albergue associated with the Cathedral, and you can go there, register, and sign up for your first night all at once. If no one is there, go to the local tourist office and ask. Everyone along the Camino is familiar with having pilgrims around who need directions. The tourist office should have all the information you need about where to go. The more information you are able to get before you leave your home, the easier it will be to get started.

When we arrived in St. Jean Pied-de-Port, our starting point, we saw no markings showing the way to the pilgrim's office. All of the literature we had read made it sound like it was obvious to go from the train station to the pilgrim's office. I was hoping this was true, because neither my husband nor I speak any French. At the time we arrived there, the streets were deserted and there was no one to ask anyway. Luckily, another pilgrim, who had arrived at the same time we did, already had her guidebook which contained a map of the small town. We were able to follow the map and find the pilgrim's office.

In retrospect, I would have liked to have had a map. Searching the internet was not useful in trying to find one. However, there are several French guide books with city maps. If this is the only city you will be traveling to in France, and, like me, you speak no French, a trip to your local library before you leave can be quite useful. Find a guidebook with a map and make a copy of the map. You might also copy any information concerning train and bus schedules to get you to St. Jean Pied-de-Port or Le Puy, another popular starting point. Public libraries have inexpensive copy machines and you will save the price of a French guidebook and buy yourself peace of mind at the same time.

In St. Jean Pied-de-Port, there is a large office to welcome pilgrims and explain the procedures. During the usual hours when pilgrims arrive, which is when the train arrives in town, the office is staffed with volunteers who speak the most common languages: Spanish, French, German and English. One volunteer will meet you at the door, determine which language you speak, and put you in a line to talk with the appropriate volunteer.

You will be given a form to fill out in your native language. (This may not be true in other cities. A Spanish phrase book may be necessary for this step.) On it you will be asked routine demographic questions such as name, home address, language, nationality and reason for taking the pilgrimage. Under reason, there are four possibilities given: religious or spiritual, cultural, physical, or other. Most people choose religious or spiritual, but to my knowledge you will not be denied a passport if you choose one of the other reasons. It also asks how you plan to accomplish the trip, by foot, by bicycle, by car or with horse or donkey. When you talk to a volunteer, they may ask a few other questions to get a feeling for why you are doing this. Our volunteer seemed curious about us, and because the office was not busy, we spent some time talking with him.

Once our volunteer was satisfied with our application, he pulled out a blank passport for each of us and entered our names and addresses on them. The passport also indicated our plan to go on foot. The current date was added and we were each asked to sign our passports. Each passport is assigned a unique number which indicates the number of pilgrims who have started from that office in that calendar year. I was number 2600 and my husband was 2601. Since January 1, 2005, 2599 other people had begun their journey from the same office. This number, along with our name and other information, was entered into a roster on a computer. This roster was subsequently sent to the pilgrim's office in Santiago and would be matched up with the number assigned to us when we completed our journey.

Our volunteer then ceremoniously took out the stamp and stamp pad for the beginning of our journey. He put the first stamp in our passport and dated it. We were now officially pilgrims.

There is a place to put the number of our US passport, which we were instructed to do before we started on the journey. At first we were reluctant, but we did enter it after the first few albergues we visited asked to see our US passport and indicated that they would not ask for it if the number had been recorded. We put our US passport numbers in our Pilgrim's Passport and our US passport went into our money belt for safekeeping and the pilgrim's passport was kept more accessible.

Both my husband and I felt like kids at Christmas as we gave the necessary information and waited patiently for the volunteer to finish the required paperwork and give us our passports. He also gave us a couple of other very valuable things: 1) a list of official, Church-run refugios (albergues or shelters) for the entire length of the Camino. 2) a map that would get us from St. Jean Pied-de-Port to Roncevalles, the first stop on the way. The walk to Roncevalles is one of the longest distances (27 kilometers) without a town or rest stop in between. He instructed us to buy something to eat along the way and to make sure we had plenty of water before starting the next day.

He assigned us to one of the refugios for the night. The Church run refugio was already full, so we were put in a private one. He gave us the name of it and told us where to find it. He pointed to a large bowl sitting on a side table in the office. It contained a pile of cockle shells, which are the traditional symbol of a pilgrim. He said we could take one and would appreciate a donation. We both looked through the shells in the bowl and we each selected one that felt right for us. We tied the shells on the back of our backpacks and there they stayed, miraculously unbroken all the way to Santiago. We left a donation and headed for our first refugio.

Upon entering, we were greeted by a cheerful voice in French. When I looked uncertain, she changed to Spanish and broken English to greet us. She asked if we wanted to take the evening meal at the refugio (at a reasonable price) and then showed us to our bunks. Our first night as pilgrims was an exciting one. We had gotten the last two beds at this particular refugio, both of which were upper bunks. Luckily, they were near each other and we could see each other for comfort.

The evening meal we signed up for turned out to be quite a feast. It was attended by other new pilgrims and two people who had already completed the pilgrimage and had come back to St. Jean Pied-de-Port to get their motorcycles and head back to their native Germany. The other new pilgrims were European with a couple of Canadians thrown in for good measure. We were the only Americans. To my surprise, most of the people spoke some English and they were surprised to find Americans on the trail. We exchanged stories about why we were doing this and a bond of friendship with all pilgrims formed. The host at the refugio was congenial and wished us all well on our journey. The meal was complete with wine and we all went to bed and slept soundly.

Each starting city has a different design for the passports issued there. The ones issued closer to Santiago do not have as many pages for stamps and each stamp has the unique symbol assigned to that particular city. Put your passport in an accessible, safe place. You will need to show it every night when you stop at an albergue. It is your most valuable possession on the trail and will be your most prized memento to take home.

Walking Stick or Staff

The walking staff is one of the most traditional symbols of a pilgrim. Most people choose to use one and I found they were not just symbolic, but downright necessary on some of the climbs. The traditional staff can be plain or intricately carved. It can be made from simple unfinished wood or highly polished, beautiful wood. We had both chosen to buy a walking staff on the Camino rather than bring one from home. St. Jean Pied-de-Port has many varieties of staffs available, priced according to their intricacy and design. A carved staff of selected wood can cost anywhere from 100 to 200 euros. One shop boasts of making staffs for more than two hundred years. They were quite beautiful and for someone who wants a unique memento, any of these would be a worthwhile purchase. However, most were out of our price range, so we continued looking. We each found a simple, but strong staff for about eight euros each.

The one thing that all the staffs had in common was a metal point at the end that would grip the earth. I thought this was rather curious until I was on the trail and found myself using the metal tip to give me more leverage as I went up and down the path.

Whether you use a staff or not is a personal preference. I do, however, recommend obtaining one. If you see one you like, buy it, as they are not always available along the way. Ask at your starting point where they can be purchased and buy it there.

Food and Water on the Trail

Planning a day or two in advance will help to insure you are not caught without water or food for long periods of time. As it was explained to us in St. Jean Pied-de-Port, the first day for us would be a long one, twenty-seven kilometers. We went looking for something to take along the next day. Bottled water was available, and we each bought a bottle that could be easily carried and accessed. This was the only bottle we bought until about half way along the trail when we accidentally walked off and left them. They were replaced in the next town. We filled these bottles along the way at the hundreds of fountains available for the pilgrims.

We also selected some fruit to take with us. We found a store that had small packets of trail mix and purchased the last two bags available. We saw other pilgrims buying bread and cheese and crackers. By the time we reached our destination, we were glad we had the trail mix and actually wished we had been able to purchase more.

St Jean Pied-de-Port is a small town in a remote region and the day we arrived, there were empty shelves in the stores. I do not know how often these stores replenish their inventory. Pilgrims starting in the next few days might have even fewer supplies to choose from. If you decide to start at Saint Jean Pied-de-Port, I would advise bringing trail mix or something like it with you. Better to have a little extra weight on the first day than to be hungry and not have the energy to climb. The first day is uphill for about three-fourths of the way.

As a general rule along the trail, we always tried to have a piece of fruit to eat along the way. There are times when there is quite a distance between cities or stores were closed in the town we were passing through. We planned for two days in advance when we could.

When you reach your destination for the day you will want something more substantial to eat. In larger cities there will be a large variety of possibilities. In smaller villages or towns, there may not be as much variety, but the quality will still be good. Look for a "Pilgrim's Menu" advertised outside an establishment. This indicates a set menu at a reasonable price. In larger cities, there is also a "Menu del Dia." This was more expensive but offered greater selections. Either way, the menu offered a salad or soup followed by an entrée of fish, chicken, beef or pork depending on the region and topped off with a piece of fruit, ice cream or pudding. There was some form of vegetable or starch available with the entrée. The meals were delicious, nutritious and inexpensive. Prices ranged from five to ten euros.

If even that amount of money seems excessive, there is another alternative. Most albergues offer kitchen facilities where the pilgrim can prepare simple food. At times the cupboards are stocked with spices and condiments, at others they are bare. If you wish to prepare something, you will have to find a store to purchase the food to be prepared. If you have not observed one as you came into the city or town, ask where one might be when you are registering at the albergue. Pasta was a pilgrim favorite. It was quick and easy and provided stamina for the next day's journey. Soup was another easy and inexpensive meal.

Before you go to the store and purchase items to prepare, take a quick look around the kitchen facilities. Look for pots, pan, dishes and implements and make sure there are sufficient items to cook what you are planning. The pots, dishes and utensils vary widely from albergue to albergue. One albergue had a very nice stove, but only one dilapidated pot and no dishes. Not much could be prepared and eaten. We ate a Pilgrim's Menu that day.

Shopping – Pharmacies, Supermarkets and Malls

Stores in Europe are different from stores in the US. In order to be able to buy things you need to know what type of store carries it. Most of the time pilgrims will be looking for food, supplies such as shampoo and soap or medicinal needs for aching muscles. Let's take a look at those types of stores.

There is no such thing as a "drug store" as it exists in the US. Spain has pharmacies (farmacias) which carry prescription drugs as well as over the counter remedies. Many items which are by prescription only in the US can be purchased over the counter at a pharmacy. These items would include common antibacterial drugs and non-addictive medications. The pharmacies are staffed by licensed pharmacists who can help you if you have an ailment. They will talk with you and diagnose your problem and sell you appropriate medication. If you know what medication you want, ask for it. It is likely they will have it or something with the same chemicals. They may not carry all the brand names that are available in the US, but they have just as many medications available. Their pharmaceutical manufacturers are just as reliable as the ones in the states. In fact, many of the products sold in the US are manufactured in Europe.

A farmacía will contain medications and medical supplies only. There may be a few cosmetics, such as body lotions in the larger pharmacies. They may also sell feminine supplies, such as tampons and sanitary napkins. If you are looking for something for a pulled muscle, a pharmacy can sell you an elastic bandage to wear and some ibuprofen cream to rub on your muscles and relieve the ache. In smaller cities or towns, not every pharmacy will be well equipped.

The term supermarket (supermercado) can be misleading to someone from the US. In the US supermarkets tend to be large with thousands of items ranging from food to automobile supplies. In Spain many supermarkets are about the size of your kitchen. I can make that statement with confidence, even knowing that many of your kitchens are quite small. Supermarkets do carry a variety of things, but not in large quantities. They will have some foodstuffs in the form of canned and packaged goods. The amount of fresh produce will vary by local availability and can be rather limited. Some of the supermarkets in larger cities are large and carry a variety of items including shampoo, body soap and laundry soap. If you are trying to find something specific, the best idea is to ask at the albergue where it can be purchased.

The concept of a mall is not widespread in Spain. The larger cities had shopping districts, but these were individual stores, usually on the ground floor of taller buildings. The upper floors might contain offices or apartments. There were department stores which carried clothes and cosmetics and sometimes shoes. Shops were more specialized, carrying a narrow assortment of items.

However, there is a mall in Santiago. It can be seen from the Camino if you know where to look as you are approaching the Cathedral. We decided to check it out one afternoon, as I was craving a new outfit after wearing the same two sets of clothes every other day for the past six weeks. If you decide to go, you will find a two story, pleasantly built mall. There are several clothing stores, eateries and miscellaneous shops. The day we were there, it was almost deserted, so we could leisurely stroll through all the shops and peruse the merchandise.

Money

When I travel I am used to using my credit cards extensively. On the Camino, most things are on a cash basis, so you will need euros. Before leaving the US we had purchased about $100 worth of euros to get us through the first few hours. When landing in Europe, we had to change planes in Frankfurt and there were opportunities to exchange money at the airport. We needed enough to take a taxi and to find something to eat for one day. Check-in at our hotel would be handled by credit card. But all albergues and restaurants on the Camino will want euros. If you have the correct change, it is even better.

Using a credit or debit card to get money is better than using travelers checks or carrying a lot of cash. ATM machines are available in larger cities. We made a habit of finding an ATM when we were in a large city and making sure we had enough cash to last until the next one. This meant taking out 200 to 300 euros each time. The ATM machines are on the same systems as the US. Check with your bank to see if the systems to access your account are used in Europe. Our bank had to make a couple of phone calls to verify the information, but we found the Cirrus and Star systems were available at all the ATMs along the Camino. Just remember to get cash in the larger cities. ATMs are not available in between.

To find an ATM, ask at the albergue. It is a common question, and they can direct you to the nearest one. You can also ask people on the street for directions to a bank. There will usually be an ATM accessible near the bank entrance.

Fountains

One of the charming things along the trail is the abundance of fountains available where pilgrims can replenish their drinking water. Fountains come in all sizes and forms. In the eastern part of the French Way, many of the fountains were simply spigots connected to underground springs. The water was sweet, fresh and delicious. Buy a bottle of water in a size easily carried and refill it as you go along.

We only encountered one fountain that had undrinkable water, and it was marked – in Spanish (no potable, no bebe). This was on the trail between Roncevalles and Zubiri. As we walked by, I remarked to my husband about the sign and what it meant. When we arrived in Zubiri, we met three young Canadian women who were traveling together. One of the women had filled her water bottle at that fountain. She spoke no Spanish and did not understand the message. When she reached the albergue, she was starting to feel ill. The attending volunteer summoned a local medic, who gave her appropriate medications, but she spent the rest of the day in her bunk with a wash cloth on her head. It was an unpleasant lesson and she learned her first few words of Spanish so this type of incident would not be repeated.

Communication and Internet

You can keep in touch with friends and family back home via the internet. Many albergues had internet kiosks located directly in the albergues. These were computers encased in a machine that accepted one euro coins. For a euro, you got 20 minutes of high speed internet access. It was wonderful. Just be careful if you are writing a long email back home. When the 20 minutes are up, they are up and the machine will cut you off. Simply make sure you have enough one euro coins to add another when your time runs low and there will not be a problem.

Many private albergues had a computer or two set up for use by pilgrims. They would post a sign asking you to respect any people waiting and not stay on line long. Most of the time computer use was free. A few times a fee was taken and other times, there was a basket for a donation.

There are also internet cafes in larger cities. Many are near the more popular albergues. The smaller cities and towns did not have access to the internet, so try to plan the timing of your communiqués.

Requirement to Obtain a Certificate of Completion

If you are walking, you only need to walk the last 100 kilometers into Santiago to fulfill the requirements to be considered a pilgrim. If this is all you want to do, the most obvious way to do this is to start 100 kilometers away from Santiago. Along the French route, the first town of any size which is located at that distance is Sarria, at 111 kilometers. Because of this fortuitous proximity, Sarria has many albergues and many pilgrims start the journey there. Sarria is a delightful town with all the modern amenities. It also has at least one special office not associated with an albergue or monastery where the pilgrim can register and obtain a pilgrim's passport for the short journey. The office is located directly on the path in an area of town which has many albergues and shops to outfit the pilgrim. Ask to be guided to the Camino coming into town, follow the arrows, and you will find the office.

If you are riding a bicycle, you must travel 200 kilometers to fulfill the requirements of a pilgrim. This would put your starting point a little west of León. The smaller towns in this area might be able to sign you up as a pilgrim, but the best idea is to start in the beautiful city of León. Since this is the starting point of many cyclists, there are many large albergues. To find one to register pilgrims, either find the Camino as it enters the city and follow it, or speak with the local tourist office and they will direct you.

Your pilgrim's passport will be your proof that you indeed covered the ground necessary for your mode of conveyance. The people who work in the Pilgrim's Office in Santiago know how long it takes to go these distances and they are familiar with the stamps of the various albergues along the way. They will inspect your pilgrim's passport and question you about your trip. Certificates of completion are not handed out lightly. Make sure you document everything correctly regarding your travels.

Traveling Solo

Many pilgrims travel alone. Often a pilgrim may begin the journey alone, and meet compatible walking companions along the way. Companions can change day by day for many reasons. One pilgrim may desire to stay at a particular place for a longer time and the others may continue. New pilgrims are met and new walking groups are formed all the time.

Walking alone is also entirely acceptable and safe. Even for single females. Let me say that again. It is perfectly safe for a woman to walk the entire Camino alone if she so desires. There is a special aura surrounding the Camino and all who walk upon it. People who live in the area will leave you alone unless you seek out conversation or need help with some problem. We met many pilgrims, both male and female, who were traveling alone. One Canadian woman, who was on the journey by herself, often walked with us when our paths and walking speed converged, which happened several times. We may have left her at a spot on the trail if she expressed the desire to stay there, only to see her again a couple of days later in front of us. It was like finding an old friend and we would spend the next few kilometers exchanging stories about what had happened during the intervening time.

Of course, common sense must prevail when traveling alone. Keep a low profile and stick to the task of completing the Camino. You will not have problems.

Symbols that Lead the Way

People who have never done any hiking or walking where it is necessary to follow a trail, often ask me how we found our way for 500 miles. A guidebook with map helped, but the guidebook was at a macro level and only gave the big picture. However, I am happy to report that the trail is well marked thanks to the work done by the Catholic Church for the 2004 and 2010 Holy Years and the efforts of the numerous volunteers in each province who maintain the Camino and all its amenities.

The Camino Frances or French Way goes through several Spanish provinces and each one has a unique way of marking the trail. The traditional symbols along the entire Camino are the yellow arrow and the cockle shell. But the way these symbols are represented is slightly different in each province. Many times a sign will contain both an arrow and a shell. The shell indicates you that you are still on the Camino and the arrow tells you the direction towards Santiago.

The trick comes in training your eye to spot the sign or symbol. They are not always obvious or close together. I seemed to see the signs better in a city, as they appeared on buildings, sidewalks and even curbs and drainage ditches. My husband was skillful at spotting them in the countryside, on a tree, in a field of tall grass, and in some areas, on irrigation aqueducts. You will develop a "searching image," which means that your brain will seek out the image amid clutter of other shapes. Once you are familiar with what to look for, it becomes easier.

As you travel along the Camino, there is a certain rhythm to the spacing of the signs. If you have gone a long distance without seeing an arrow or a shell or another pilgrim, it is a good time to stop and ask someone if you are still on the right track. Many days it was not necessary to see any signs. We only had to look ahead to see other pilgrims and we followed them.

We did experience missing a sign and somehow got off the Camino. We were entering Burgos, which is a large metropolitan area. Our guidebook showed a rather lengthy lead into the city, then a sharp turn to the right, followed by a quick left. We never found those turns. For several city blocks, we searched for a symbol to assure us we were on the correct street. We did not find one. We planned to spend the night there and according to the guidebook, the albergue was on the far side of the city. We were not sure we would find it if we continued without a trail sign. Our situation was further complicated because it was a Sunday, so stores were closed and the city was deserted. We attempted to locate landmarks shown in the guidebook, but were unsuccessful.

We decided to turn right, thinking that we were walking parallel to the Camino and had just missed the turnoff. When we did this, the area became more populated and we were able to stop a family on their way out of their apartment and ask just where we were. They were very helpful and put us back in the direction we had just come from. As it turned out, we did not miss the turnoff, we had not reached it yet. Our guidebook underestimated (or we overestimated) the length of the street leading into the city. We were not even on the map yet. After asking a couple more people as we continued, we were able to find a yellow arrow which put us back on the path to the albergue.

Backpack Transport

There are times in life when one needs help. There is a service on some parts of the Camino to transport your backpack to a predetermined place so you can walk without carrying any weight. There were notices on the bulletin boards of some albergues to advertise this service. This could be useful for someone who has suffered a minor injury and can walk but not carry a pack. It could be useful for someone with a minor handicap, who could handle the terrain, if no weight had to be carried. And it is also useful for people who, for whatever reason, do not wish to carry a pack, but want to experience walking along the Camino.

A call to a phone number advertising the service will get this process in motion. You will be quoted a price, based on the number of backpacks and the distance you want them transported. If an agreement is reached, the proprietors of the albergue where you are staying are notified. In the morning, the pilgrims pack their backpacks and leave them in an agreed upon place in the albergue. Identification is put on the bags indicating where they are to be taken. The proprietor will give the transport service the bags. The pilgrims leave and start walking.   At some time during the morning, the service arrives and picks up the bags. They may also be dropping off bags from another albergue further back.   The new bags are taken to the destination albergue and will be there when the pilgrims arrive later in the day.

We did not use this service, but saw others taking advantage of it. We witnessed the picking up and dropping off a couple of times.   The service seemed rapid and efficient.

Rituals for the Pilgrim in the Cathedral de Santiago de Compostela

Pilgrims have been arriving in Santiago for hundreds of years. The Cathedral has undergone spectacular expansion and certain rituals have evolved. We learned about these only when we entered the city and stopped at an albergue on the outskirts of Santiago to walk the final three kilometers without our backpack. We met a fellow pilgrim from Canada who we had walked with for several days at various points along the way. She had arrived three days ahead of us and had spent the time exploring the city.   Someone had told her about the rituals and she passed the information on to us. I had not read about them in any literature and was delighted to be informed at this precise moment. We eagerly listened, then cleaned up for the day, and started our final three kilometers of the journey.

The now familiar shells led us to the Cathedral. It is huge, with many entrances. You want to find the Portico de la Gloria, but if it is not the first place you encounter, just keep walking around and you will eventually find it. It is directly opposite the main altar and there will probably be a line of pilgrims waiting to perform the first ritual. Get in line so you can experience it.

The art in the Cathedral is overwhelmingly beautiful and the Portico de la Gloria is one of the masterpieces of Compostela Romanesque art. The central column contains a sculpture of Saint James and this is where you will stand for the first ritual. As you stand in front of the column, place your hands on it and make a wish. Saint James grants the wishes of pilgrims. On the day we arrived, there were several people in line ahead of us and several behind us. When it was my turn, I casually placed my hands on the column and to my surprise, I felt a surge of energy. It was so overwhelming that I forgot to make a wish – I just stood there absorbing it. I would have liked to have stayed longer, but others were waiting and I know the surge I received was not only from Saint James, but from all the other pilgrims who had been there throughout the ages. I wanted others to experience it also.

Right behind the column is a much smaller statue of the master craftsman, Mateo, who created the statue of Saint James and all the other sculpture in this portico. He was so vain about the magnificence of his work, he put in an image of himself. Because of his vanity and pride, he was condemned never to see the final product. Various accounts have him going blind or dying, but he did not view it. This brings us to the second ritual. Stand in front of the statue of Mateo and knock heads with him three times. This will give the pilgrim some of his illustrious intelligence and artistry without the vanity and pride.

The third traditional ritual involves going to the main altar of the Church and embracing the gilded and bejeweled likeness of Saint James above the casket containing his remains. This is done from the back of the image. The Church has provided a walkway behind the altar so the pilgrim can walk up to the image and embrace it from the rear. The figurine is made of gold and precious stones and this ritual is monitored by someone affiliated with the Church, who stands by discretely as pilgrims perform the ritual. I did not get the same reaction during this ritual as I did with the first.

After embracing the golden image, pilgrims walk down a stairway below the altar to see the small silver casket containing the remains of Saint James. It is beautifully crafted and seems quite simple and austere when compared to the elaborate cathedral surrounding it and the arduous journey that most have taken to see it. Maybe that is the point.

Following the third ritual, we sat in the main section of the Cathedral to watch the activity around us and take in the realization that we were actually in Santiago. As we sat facing the altar, other pilgrims were performing the third ritual. We could not see the individual pilgrims, only their arms as they embraced St. James. It gave a surreal quality to the surroundings as the image seemed to have signs of life with the moving arms. Each pilgrim's embrace was different; some were quick and efficient, others graceful and lingering.

These rituals are a way to bring closure to the journey and they did just that for me. I felt as if I had accomplished the goal I set out for myself six weeks earlier, but I was also sad because the journey was over. I was now free of the routine formed along the trail. I did not realize it at the time, but I would come to miss that simple routine.

Completing the Camino

The Pilgrim's Office is located at Rúa do Vilar 1, next to the Cathedral. (Phone 981562419) As you enter the city, the arrows and shells continue to point the way. The sign for the office is inconspicuous and it can be missed unless there is a line of pilgrims waiting to check in. Ask anyone in any of the shops around the Cathedral and they can point you to the Pilgrims Office. The day we arrived, no line existed and we were able to go right up to the counter.

When you walk off the street into the Pilgrim's Office, it looks more like a tourist office than anything else. On your left is a counter with two or three people busy at computers. Bus, train and plane schedules are posted on the wall. These wonderful people will help you arrange transportation back to your starting point. If you are going back by plane and you have a valid completion certificate, you will only pay half fare. But you must arrange it at this desk and copies of your completed certificate must be turned in. This is one way Spain and the Spanish airlines recognize the importance of the pilgrimage. Bus and train tickets are not discounted, but are reasonably priced and the people here will also help with your specific arrangements.

Directly across from the travel counter is a counter selling various official mementos. Among these are DVDs and VHS tapes about the Camino and Santiago. If you purchase a DVD, remember to ask for the specific region and related version compatible with DVD players in your country. I do not know if various regions are actually available as I did not even think about it and I now have a region 2 (Europe) DVD about the Camino. It will not play in my DVD player, but it does play on my computer. I do not mind watching it on the computer, but I would like to be able to view it on the larger screen of my television.

But these two counters will not be your focus when you first enter. The actual office is on the second floor. Go up the stairs straight ahead and turn left and you will find a large room with a long counter spanning the entire length of the room. There will be several people behind the counter waiting at their computers. The day we arrived the office was practically empty and we went right up to the desk. A young woman closely examined our pilgrim's passport with all the stamps and dates. She asked if we had walked all the way or had taken a bus or some other form of transportation part of the way. We truthfully replied that we had walked every step and she seemed pleased. She had a demeanor that said she could detect any lie we might have made. She then got out certificates to fill in our names and put us on the official roster of pilgrims who have completed the requirements.

An interesting thing then happened. She looked at my husband's first name, Richard, and transformed it into the Latin version, Richardum, and wrote it on his certificate. She looked at my name, Cheri, and asked me what other name was associated with it. I told her it was not a nickname, but my given name and I did not know of another version. She did not seem certain what to put on the certificate. She consulted another person and they had a lively discussion about the possible derivation of my name. They came up blank - so my actual name is on my certificate. Our last name of Powell went on the certificate unchanged. I asked why they used the Latin version of names and was told that it has always been the tradition to do so. I had not read anything about this anywhere else.

She handed us our certificates and our journey was officially over. I did request one further thing. The previous year (2004) had been a Holy Year and special tubes had been made to hold the certificates and keep them from being crushed. I had heard there were quite a few left over and so I asked if I might have one. They did indeed have some, so for one euro I was able to put both our certificates in a container safe from tearing or crushing. Ask for a container as they might have started making them on a regular basis.

Tip #5 Takeaways

- ❖ There are many types of accommodations to satisfy every pilgrim.

- ❖ Get your Pilgrims's Passport at a larger city.

❖ There is abundant food and water on the Camino.

❖ Make sure you have cash for albergues and shops in smaller towns.

❖ Fountains along the way have drinkable water unless specifically marked.

❖ The internet is available in some albergues and in internet cafes in towns.

❖ It is safe to travel alone.

❖ The Camino is well marked.

Tip #6

Know the Etiquette on the Path
and
in the Albergues

Manners are a sensitive awareness of the feelings of others. If you have that awareness, you have good manners, no matter which fork you use. Emily Post

Politeness and consideration for others is like investing pennies and getting dollars back.
Thomas Sowell

Every culture has a set of "rules," whether they are written down or handed down by example. The Camino is unique and international and has developed an informal set of rules of its own.

Tip #6 Know the Etiquette on the Path and in the Albergues

The American Heritage dictionary defines etiquette as "The practices and forms prescribed by social convention or by authority." Newspaper advice columnists have sometimes reduced the definition to "behavior that makes others comfortable." This second definition is closer to the philosophy prevalent along the Camino. Because there is a coming together of so many different nationalities, languages and customs an undeniable etiquette has evolved that attempts to make everyone comfortable. It is derived from local customs and the activity Pilgrims have undertaken: a pilgrimage. In order for it to be effective, everyone must take part.

If you are not a Spaniard, then you are a guest in the country of the Camino. Some knowledge or appreciation for Spanish customs and traditions should be observed. There are several internet links in **Appendix D** with excellent advice concerning Spanish customs. Some of the links are oriented toward a business environment, but what is true in business often holds true in a social environment. As there is extensive information on Spanish traditions on the internet and in many books, I will let the reader explore those places. The rest of this chapter refers specifically to the Camino.

On the Path

Everyone has their own pace when walking. Some pilgrims will be passing others and some pilgrims will be passed. Luckily, everyone along the path is going in the same direction, so there is a common purpose and no need to worry about getting out of the way for people going back. The most common greeting along the path is "Buen Camino!" which literally means "Good way!" or "Good path!" but can more emotionally be translated as "I hope you have a wonderful journey as you make your way along the Camino!" It is said with enthusiasm and the proper response is also "Buen Camino!"

Another greeting said to be common by several web sites is "Ultreya!" which means "Forward!" or "Onward!" but I only heard this used once during the entire length of the Camino. It is a cry of encouragement and maybe I did not look like I needed much encouragement as I went along. It would be a good idea to keep both of these phrases in mind as one meets others along the trail.

Because pilgrims come from so many different backgrounds, it does not hurt to be able to give traditional greetings in the native tongue of the recipient. There were days when we started the walk and shouted out "Buenas dias!" "Guten morgan!" "Bon jour!" and/or "Good morning!" to the appropriate pilgrim. They either replied in their language or in ours. We had learned the nationality of the individuals during the previous afternoon and it was nice to be able to greet them in their native tongue, even if our pronunciation was not perfect and they were the only words we knew in their language. It gave a cheerful start to the day for everyone.

The width of the path varies from a single file cow path to a wide paved road. There are groups of people, couples and singles walking along. Some are talking, others are silent. Some are walking leisurely; others are keeping a brisk pace. Some are taking in the sights, be it in a city or countryside and others are walking with a purpose and destination in mind. Sometimes there will be no one in sight. Sometimes there will be a crowd. The idea is to respect what other pilgrims are doing and let them do it.

Sometimes this can be difficult if you are in the mood for internal reflection and everyone around is talking. If you can take yourself physically away from the distraction, do it. If they are walking slowly, speed up and find solitude. If they are walking quickly, slow up and they will soon be far ahead. If your traveling companions are talking and you want to leisurely stroll, arrange a meeting point up ahead and let them walk on. Everyone will be much more relaxed if the daily process does not turn into a race among pilgrims.

If you are the leisurely walker, be aware of others approaching from behind you, and when they reach you, step to the right and let them pass. This is an ideal time for a hearty, "Buen Camino!" You will get a smile and the same greeting given back to you.

Along much of the Camino the path for walking pilgrims and bicycle riding pilgrims is the same. This can cause a clash when speedy bicycles overtake walking pilgrims. If you are walking, be alert for the possibility of a bicycle and as they approach, step to the RIGHT so they can pass on the left. If you are riding a bicycle, be aware that walking pilgrims may not always be aware of your approach. Make some kind of noise! Greet with a "Buen Camino!" and the path will open for you as the walkers respond and get out of your way.

We found most bicyclists to be courteous and respectful of our slower walking pace. There were occasional surprises when the path was narrow and their approach was fast. When this occurred, we scrambled for someplace to go. On one occasion I almost took a dip in a creek when a rapidly-moving, quiet cyclist bumped against me as I attempted to get out of his way. It did not alter his advancement and I was off the path looking back down the trail for any companions. Bicyclists usually travel in groups. As a walker, if you have stepped aside for one, check for others not far behind.

Downhill paths can be especially treacherous when walkers and cyclists are together. Cyclists tend to try to gain maximum speed for any upcoming uphill. Walking pilgrims can be an impediment to that goal. The best compromise occurs when the walking pilgrims are aware of the oncoming cyclists. A bell, a horn or some way for the cyclists to make noise will allow walkers to step aside in a timely fashion.

If the path is wide and flat and busy, it can seem as if traffic signals are needed. Neither walkers nor cyclists should take up the entire width. A row of cyclists approaching at even a moderate pace can quicken the heartbeat of a walker who must take several steps to the side of the path to get out of the way.

Do not litter along the Camino. This may seem like an obvious thing to say, but we did see some litter. As we approached Santiago, and were within the 100 kilometer requirement for walking pilgrims, litter became evident and even pervasive in some places. If you are munching on something that came out of a wrapper, put the wrapper in a pocket until it can be discarded at the next town or albergue.

Do not create graffiti. We did not see any on the early part of the trail. As we neared Santiago the arrows and signs along the way became strewn with notes, pictures and comments. If you must communicate with someone who is behind you on the trail, leave a note at a predefined albergue or restaurant.   Some albergues have bulletin boards for that purpose. In several places there were murals depicting some form of pilgrim activity. These were well done, inspiring and sometimes amusing. If you have artistic ability, consider volunteering your talents in a more acceptable and organized way. Other pilgrims will appreciate it.

In the Albergues

At the end of the day all pilgrims bed down together in some albergue. This puts pilgrims in the closest proximity to each other than they will experience on the trail.   There are different people every day. Sometimes beds are so close together there is little room for personal items. It is at times like these, when etiquette and consideration for others is needed most.

Many albergues do not unlock the doors until some time in the afternoon. This can be anytime from 1:00 to 4:00 or even 5:00 in the evening. If you arrive before the albergue is ready to receive you, it can be tiring waiting in line. With many pilgrims on the road, the competition for beds can be fierce. If you arrive early and want to stay at a particular albergue, you must reserve your place in line for registration. This is usually done using the backpacks as place markers. The first person to arrive will take off his pack and lean it against the door to the albergue. The next person will put their pack immediately behind. The next person's pack behind that, and so on, until the line is represented by the packs. You can then find a shady spot to relax until the albergue opens. When it does open, everyone will return, claim their pack and enter in an orderly fashion to register.

This procedure was followed at several albergues as we neared Santiago. If you are traveling with companions, and desire to explore while waiting, leave one person to watch the packs. We had no reservation leaving the packs inside the albergue once we were registered, but on the outside, the packs were visible to all who passed, both pilgrim and non-pilgrim. We did not want to tempt anyone by leaving them unattended. If other pilgrims were lounging about and waiting also, we might strike up a conversation and ask them to keep an eye out while we ran a quick errand. Everyone we asked in this manner was happy to help and we returned the favor for other pilgrims. Waiting for albergues to open can be a good time to meet some of the other travelers and enjoy some conversation.

There is also a priority for the manner in which pilgrims are accepted at albergues. All walking pilgrims will be taken in before bicycle riding pilgrims. Walking pilgrims tend to stop earlier in the day. In most albergues registration for walkers is open as soon as the albergue is available for the day. Any bicyclist must wait until a later time. At around 7:00PM, a bicyclist may register, claim a bed and begin his or her own routine. This rule is strictest in the church run albergues.

Some privately owned albergues will take the cyclists earlier. The system works well because the cyclists want to cover as much territory as possible in one day and will ride until nearly sunset. I know of one bike riding pilgrim who completed the entire 500 miles in eleven days!

Some albergues assign beds, others allow you to choose. If beds are being assigned, graciously take whatever has been assigned to you. Usually groups and couples are taken into consideration and assignments made accordingly. If, for whatever reason you are not happy with the bed assigned to you, try to accept it and make do. Most albergues, even the privately owned ones, are run by volunteers. They try to please, and theirs is a thankless job. Just think about what you would be paying to stay in a hotel. Compare the facilities and value of what you are receiving. And it is only for one night.

In albergues where you choose your bed, do so by placing your backpack on it. That effectively "stakes a claim" for that area for the night. Many times we would register at the albergue, hastily claim our beds with our packs and then go out in search of something to eat. No need to unpack any further. The sight of a backpack on a bed is enough.

Respect the space around a bed as belonging to that bed. This is relatively simple if you have the lower bunk. If you are in the upper bunk and a stranger has the lower one, you will have to share floor space. The lower bunks are taken first and the upper ones are only filled by latecomers. If you find yourself on the upper bunk with the lower already claimed, note where the belongings of that pilgrim are located. If they have been placed at the side of the bed, then place your belongings at the foot of the bed. Your backpack will still go on the upper bunk to initially claim it. Everyone understands the need to keep belongings in some sort of order, and an area of ownership quickly emerges.

While at the albergue you will be unpacking to find toiletries and fresh clothes. Most pilgrims spread their things on the bed for use while it is still daylight. If you are in the upper bunk, this may mean climbing up on the bunk to arrange your possessions in a usable order. Before retiring for the night, pack up things that you will not immediately need when getting up.

There are limited laundry facilities and bath rooms at all albergues. Usually this is not a problem as pilgrims arrive at different times and use the facilities as they are available. In the morning there can sometimes be a bottleneck in the bathrooms if everyone wants to brush their teeth at once. If you sense many in the room are getting up at the same time, it might be a good idea to roll over and catch a few more snoozes until they are gone.

Sunny days can produce a rush to the laundry as pilgrims want to wash their extra clothes and bed linens. This can mean waiting for use of the sinks and crowding on the clothes line. Be creative if this occurs. Nearby trees or bushes will give adequate support to most clothing. If you brought extra string or a small plastic clothesline, this is the time to bring it out.

Be self sufficient. Do not ask to borrow clothes pins or use another pilgrim's laundry soap, shampoo or other items. Everyone has calculated what they will need on the trip and is carrying the necessities. If you honestly thought you had enough shampoo for a week and ran out in five days, talk with the person running the albergue for help. They can recommend a nearby store, or in some cases, they will help you from their own personal homes. There is not enough good to say about the wonderful people who run the albergues. They go out of their way to help pilgrims in need.

Bath areas are shared by all pilgrims. After pilgrims leave for the day, volunteers clean the areas and make the entire albergue ready for the next day's influx of pilgrims. When you leave the bathroom after washing, clean up the area for others who will be using it. In showers, try to keep the water as contained in the shower area as possible. Water strewn about an area is unpleasant for another person coming in. Sinks can be rinsed so soap and dirt go down the drain. Think about how you would like to find the bath area and leave it accordingly.

If the bathrooms are not co-ed, but are separated by sex, respect that. One morning while bathing, I was surprised by a man in the woman's bathroom. I asked him what he was doing there and he said he was in a hurry and the men's room was busy. Please. Have a little respect and follow the rules set up by the albergue.

Many pilgrims want to take a siesta or nap in the afternoon. The hours from about 3:00PM to 5:00PM are when the stores and restaurants close, so it is a good time to relax from the day's journey and maybe even sleep. This time of day sees many pilgrims curled up on their bunks writing in their journals or just curled up relaxing or even sleeping. Respect the quiet of the sleeping, and if you want to engage in conversation, review the videos you shot today (complete with sound), or do any other noise-making activity, do so in the dining room, laundry room or outside the building. All albergues had some place where pilgrims could go for conversation. Go to a restaurant and have a glass of wine. Respect the pilgrims who are relaxing in the sleeping room and do not make noise there.

As the day draws to a close, pilgrims will start to bed down for the night. Try to get your re-packing done during the daylight hours. Most albergues have a "lights out" time posted in the entrance to the albergue or sleeping room. When this time comes, the lights are turned off and pilgrims are expected to go to sleep for the night. Most pilgrims are eager to fall asleep. Do not get out your flashlight and begin reading a book or writing a letter. This is especially rude to everyone in the room. The light is distracting, no matter how small the flashlight. Plan your time to read an important book or write a letter during daylight hours.

Lights out is also the time to cease conversations. Voices carry quite well in the closed environment of the sleeping rooms and other pilgrims do not want to hear about your adventures. Even conversations whispered to a person in the next bunk will be overhead by someone on the other side of the room.

No one can completely control snoring. However, there are some things that can be done to lessen the intensity and volume. If you know that you do snore, check with your doctor before leaving home for some possible remedies and aids. Some over-the-counter items can help. Do a Google search on "stop snoring" and you will have many sites to investigate. Medical technology has advanced in these areas also, and there may be things available today that were unheard of in the past. You may be charmed by your partner's snoring sonata, but strangers sleeping in the same room will not be enchanted. Inform your partner if this might be a problem.

I spent many sleepless nights when my husband and I first married. I would lie awake and listen to various sounds and then complete silence for a few seconds. This was followed by gasps for air and a return to snoring sounds. This went on in cycles every few minutes. I had read about sleep apnea, and I asked my husband if he had ever had been checked out for it. He had not, but soon set up an appointment with a local sleep clinic that confirmed his sleep apnea. To correct the problem, he underwent outpatient surgery and now the apnea is gone and his snoring is infrequent. Insurance covered all the procedures and recovery was rapid. He now seems to snore only when he has eaten dairy products during the day, especially ice cream. I have not checked with a doctor concerning this cause and effect. It is just an observation made over the years. Sometimes solutions are very simple.

There was one particular night in an albergue when the snoring was memorable. We were in a small room with eight bunks. Everyone in the room was part of a couple and most of the men were on top bunks and women on the bottom. As one gentleman dozed off for the night, his snoring began to rattle the rafters. Everyone else in the room was awake as evidenced by the tossing and turning heard from each bed. Finally one pilgrim could stand it no longer. He spoke to the wife and asked her if this would continue all night, and if anything could be done about it. She sheepishly replied that he was very tired, but that some sleeping positions might relieve the situation. She woke him and pushed him over on his side. He seemed to realize what had happened and rearranged his body in a position where the snoring would be lessened. It worked and we were all able to get some much needed rest. We subsequently saw this couple again in another albergue and specifically chose beds in a different room.

The biggest complaint I heard from pilgrims concerning the behavior of others involves plastic bags. Many pilgrims used plastic shopping bags to wrap around items for packing. These are the ubiquitous bags used at grocery stores, discount stores and clothing stores. Stores in Spain are no exception. When you buy the fruit for tomorrow's journey, it will probably be put in a plastic bag. During the day the noise made by removing an object or wrapping around an object is not evident. However, in the early morning when there is relative silence, the rustling of these bags can sound like a stampede of small animals running through the albergue.

If possible, pack the items in a plastic bag the night before. Or take the items to be packed outside the sleeping room before wrapping and stashing them. ZipLoc bags use a heavier plastic and do not make as much noise, but there is still some. Ideally, at least for the pilgrim still sleeping, items requiring waterproofing could be wrapped in pliant oilcloth and packed in silence. Alas, oilcloth is heavy and cumbersome and not destined to become the favorite of pilgrims. For those who must rise early and pack, be aware of the ramifications of your movements on others and strive to be a silent as possible.

If you do get up before the sun, do not turn on the light. It will wake others. This may seem like a no-brainer, but some pilgrims are in their own universe and blissfully unaware of the consequences of light in a darkened room full of sleeping people. It happened to us very early one morning. The light was turned on in a room of about 30 pilgrims. Even groans of dismay from pilgrims disturbed by the light did not produce realization in the pilgrims who had turned it on. It was only when a just awakened pilgrim went over and turned out the light that the offending parties realized something was amiss. However, the light-supplying pilgrims thought it was rude of the other to turn off the lights because they had trouble seeing. Duh! Not to be suppressed, they produced flashlights to continue their packing and noisy exit. It was 4:30AM. I know because I looked at my watch in disbelief when the lights were on. I wonder to this day how the early risers can see the markers on the trail before sunrise.

Modern technology has brought cell phones to most people. A problem is produced when pilgrims bring them along on this journey and use them as alarm clocks. The charming ring-tones you have chosen to alert you to a call do not seem at all charming while sleeping. If you must have your phone with you, turn off the capability to receive calls and put it on vibrate to wake you up. Relatives and friends in different time zones may not realize they are calling you in the middle of the night in your local time.   If someone is trying to get in touch with you because of an emergency, there is nothing that can be done in the middle of the night and by having the phone turned off you will have a missed call message to follow up on the next morning.

Alarm clocks on watches and cell phones are designed to be just that: alarming. If you are a heavy sleeper and want to get up early, you may normally set your alarm to be quite loud. Even a beep on a low setting will wake a light sleeper across the room. If you desire to be out the door early and you need an alarm, find something that can be set to vibrate and placed in the bed with you. Your relationship with other pilgrims will be much better.

On a journey that involves a large amount of physical endurance, most people do not smoke. As we neared Santiago and the physical demands were lessened, we did encounter a few people who had the need to light up. Albergues are implicit no-smoking areas. But there is always plenty of outdoors for the smoker. Please restrict any smoking to the outdoor areas.

A Final Thought

Everyone has their own reason for wanting to experience the Camino. Be aware and have enough respect to allow others their experience. Be assertive enough so others will respond and do the same for you. It is a delicate balance.

Tip #6 Takeaways

❖ Be kind to your fellow pilgrim.

Tip #7

Know How to Stay Healthy on the Camino

Health is not valued till sickness comes.
Dr. Thomas Fuller

The sum of the whole is this: walk and be happy; walk and be
healthy. The best way to lengthen out our days is to walk steadily
and with a purpose.
Charles Dickens

Walking the Camino can take its toll. Even the most well prepared pilgrim can fall prey to sickness or an injury. Knowing what to do will help ease any negative consequences.

Tip #7 – Know How to Stay Healthy on the Camino

Deaths on the Camino

On average, three pilgrims die each year on the Camino. You probably read the last sentence twice. Yes, it is true. It is a statistic that both shocked and saddened me when I heard it. The cause of each pilgrim's death is not published as far as I know, but several shrines can be seen along the length of the Camino in tribute to a few who have died along the way. Sometimes these shrines will contain a brief story telling about the pilgrims and how they died. Others are simply silent monuments. But if we extrapolate information from what is given, we will have insight into the other deaths and warning signs and precautions that should be taken.

There is one monument to a young woman who was killed by a car outside of a large city. She had been walking with friends and apparently not paying attention when crossing a street. In many places, the Camino crosses major intersections or goes along a major highway with cars and trucks traveling at highway speeds. Pilgrims must walk single file and should be alert to any lack of alertness on the part of oncoming drivers. Most drivers try to be courteous and watch out for pilgrims, but things can happen quickly at high speeds. When you find yourself walking along major highways, pay attention to the traffic - as well as to the signs along the Camino.

Within the 100 kilometer marker, there are several shrines to pilgrims who passed away due to health related problems. Many pilgrims undertake the Camino later in life when they have been freed from other responsibilities and now have the time and money to undertake the journey they have been thinking about during their entire lives. Unfortunately, this may also be when these pilgrims were not in the best of health to begin with. Whatever the state of your health when you decide to go, know your limitations and make sure you have sufficient medication to handle any existing conditions. If you have not been physically active for many years, the exertion of walking every day can bring more of a toll than a benefit to your body. Use common sense.

If you know you have a handicap or condition that will make it difficult for you to walk the required distance, choose the places where you will walk. Some of the Camino is flat. Some of it is quite steep and challenging. Take a bus over this section if it will be difficult for you. Know the terrain and plan accordingly.

If you are healthy and alert, what else is there to consider? Reread **Tip #2** and make sure you have packed sunscreen, bug repellent, supplements you normally take and any prescription medications. Make sure your footgear is broken in and it will be comfortable on all the terrain you will travel.

Make sure you always have a bottle of water with you. The food in restaurants and bars is excellent and there should not be a problem eating anything that looks good to you.

Sometimes you will be ill for reasons out of your control – changes in the weather, catching a bug from another pilgrim or overexertion. If you feel the need for professional medical attention, ask at any albergue. Someone there will be able to put you in touch with some type of medical professional. It may be a pharmacist or a doctor who volunteers to help pilgrims. There may or may not be a charge. If the situation looks serious, the volunteers at the albergue will help you find the assistance you need.

Accidents and Insurance

In the event of an accident or something which requires more intervention, medical insurance may be needed. This is something you need to make arrangements for when you are making your plans to get to Spain. Insurance in the US is not usable outside the US borders, so supplemental insurance should be purchased. If you are using a travel agent, they can show you policies good for the duration of your trip. Benefits vary from policy to policy, so read the fine print carefully before you go.

We purchased our tickets from an on-line auction, SkyAuction (See **Appendix D**) and purchased a health plan along with our ticket. If you are not using a service to purchase your transportation tickets, do a Google search for "travel health insurance" and you will get a list of companies to investigate. You might also check with your stateside health insurance agency to see if they offer a travel package.

Wherever you decide to get insurance, make sure you know how to contact someone while in Spain. It does not do much good to have insurance if you do not know how to make use of it when needed. This means contact phone numbers and the names of institutions that will accept your policy. Keep this important information in the same place you keep your passport and credit cards.

Tip #7 Takeaways

- ❖ Carry basic first aid.

- ❖ Make sure you have sufficient amounts of prescription medication you take.

- ❖ Carry an extra pair of prescription glasses.

Appendix A

A Typical Day

A Typical Day

In the pre-dawn morning, I am aroused from my slumber by a beeping noise coming from somewhere in the room. It is a pilgrim who wants to be on the trail before sunup and has inadvertently awoken most of the other pilgrims.   I roll over and attempt to ignore the subsequent rustling noises as the early rising pilgrim places items in plastic bags and returns them to backpacks for the day's journey. Each zipper on a backpack proclaims its readiness with a loud "zip!" sound as the pilgrim stuffs articles in appropriate pockets and closes them.

I do not even attempt to look at my watch. If there is not enough natural light to see, it is too early to get up. For the next hour and a half or so, I am in and out of sleep as more pilgrims awake and get ready for the trail. Soon there is enough light and I glance at my watch - 6:12 AM. Time to get started for the day.

I lean over to the bed pushed up against mine and gently nudge my husband.   As in most albergues, the beds provided are bunk beds and in this particular one, there are a few that have been pushed together so couples may each have a bottom or top bed in close proximity to their partner.   We had chosen a pair of bottom bunks on the previous afternoon. My husband glances at me through sleep filled eyes and without a word between us, starts his day too.

As I swing my feet to the floor, I slip on my flip-flops and grab my Ziploc bags containing my facial wash, soap, toothbrush and tooth soap. I also locate my comb, wash cloth, towel and, if necessary, tissues and I head to the bathroom.   As I look around the room, some pilgrims are still sleeping, but there are also many empty beds which have been vacated by the early risers. I try to walk quietly in my flip-flops, making sure they do not make noise to wake other pilgrims who may still want a few extra minutes of peaceful sleep.

I have slept in the shorts, top and underwear I will be wearing, so no dressing is necessary. In the bathroom, I wash my face, brush my teeth, run a comb through my hair and apply a facial moisturizer. I find an unused toilet stall and take care of that necessity. I then assess myself in the mirror and adjust my clothing as needed. Not bad. I am ready for the day.

I go back into the sleeping room and discover my husband gathering up our belongings. I take my pillow case off the pillow provided and begin to stuff my sleeping bag, my silk sleep sack and the pillow case in the stuff sack for the sleeping bag. I put the actual bag in first and the silk pillow case and sleep sack in last so they will be on top in case the bag is not needed when we stop tonight. Everything fits nicely and this can be done with a minimum of noise. I glance around the room and see we have not disturbed the remaining sleeping pilgrims.

I locate my fanny pack just where I left it: wrapped around part of the headboard in such a way that anyone trying to take it would wake me up. While sleeping, we put our money belts in our respective fanny packs and either put them between us when we are in beds side by side, or somehow hook them around part of the bed so removal by another person would be noticed and stopped. We did not have any problems, but were more secure taking a few precautions with the few valuables we had with us. I take out my money belt and discretely put it on, sliding it below the waist of my shorts. It rides there comfortably, giving me a feeling of well being knowing my valuables are safe.

I find my socks that I had laid out the night before. Before putting them on, I rub a little ibuprofen cream on my feet to ease any aches. It feels good as I slip on the socks and sandals. I gather my toiletries and put them in the appropriate pockets in my backpack. The previous evening before retiring, I packed everything I would not immediately need when I got up, so my time and noise in gathering everything would be minimal.   I sling my sleeping bag over one shoulder, grab my fanny pack, backpack and staff and head out of the room.

Outside the sleeping room we secure everything in the backpacks and make sure all zippers are closed. I reach in a pocket in the backpack where I keep frequently needed things and I pull out the bottle of sunscreen. Although it is early, I put a light coat on my legs, arms, neck and face.   My husband does the same. It is now time to suit up and begin walking. I put on my fanny pack first, securing it so the contents are in front for easy access.   I then put on my backpack and adjust any loose straps from the previous day.   The pack settles in comfortably against my body as the weight is distributed to my hips.

My husband and I glance at each other to make sure we have not forgotten anything. Up to this point, we have not spoken, but only executed our usual morning routine to get us on the road. We check our water bottles for sufficient water for the morning and we each grab our staff and leave the albergue to start walking.

We look around to find the arrows which point us in the right direction. Most mornings are delightful with crisp air that brings us to full consciousness.   Some albergues offer coffee and bread to get the pilgrims going.   Most do not, so about 10:00 AM we start to look for a bar. No, not to start drinking, but to get a bocadillo which is a sandwich made with wonderful French bread, ham or cheese.   This also gives us a chance to rest for a few minutes and recharge our energy.

One of the most enchanting things on the path is the wildflowers. There seem to be no weeds in this part of Spain, only fields of crops, mostly grapes, and flowers. It is as if every part of the countryside has been manicured and the flowers are part of a grand gardening scheme. The most common flower is the red poppy and I am delighted each day as the poppies line the pathway and seem to brighten our day.

Along the way, there are frequent fountains with drinkable water and we use these to replenish our water bottles. These fountains have been placed along the Camino specifically for the pilgrims. In the mountainous regions, the fountains are connected to underground springs which offer the most delicious tasting water in the world.

The day before we had mapped the distance we want to go today. We always had a secondary plan in case the weather was bad, we were especially tired, or we found something interesting not mentioned in the guide book. Most days we follow the plan we had set out. We try to time it so we reach our desired destination around 1:00 to 3:00PM. Then we start looking for an albergue. The guidebook, combined with the original list from St. Jean Pied-de-Port, provides us with the number of albergues in a particular place. Once there, we are on the lookout for signs pointing to the actual albergues. There are many directly on the Camino, but others are located just a short distance away. Albergue owners know that tired pilgrims will take the first acceptable place, and being too far off the route is a definite disadvantage.

We find an albergue and walk in. The door is open but no one is in attendance. We notice a sign next to the door. Someone will be by around 5:00 PM to collect the fee and stamp our credentials. We are instructed to choose a bed and make ourselves at home. The albergue we have chosen on this day appears to be an old school, remodeled to accommodate travelers. There are two large rooms that were classrooms in their previous lives, as evidenced by the chalk boards still usable at one end of the room. But now there is a row of bunk beds along each of the walls. Each room is large enough to have ten bunks along each wall perpendicular to the chalk board. There is also a row of windows on the outer wall with push out openings at the bottom. There are no curtains at the windows.

Since we are the first to arrive, we have the prime choice of beds. Our minds begin to whirl as we asses the relative advantages of the rooms and bed locations. The building is facing east, so the room in the front, with no curtains at the windows will get the morning sun first and be bright. We choose the back room to delay the brightness. In this room there is a row of bunks along the inside wall and another row along the windows with the head of the beds directly at the windows. We consider temperature and the availability of having fresh air and decide to take a bed along the windows. We choose the far end of the row, away from the door, as there are usually other pilgrims who wake before we do and the closer they are to the door, the less noise there will be for us. Choosing the end bed also gives more room to spread out our belongings while we are there. This particular albergue has chairs between the beds, so pilgrims do not have to sit on the beds to take off and put on their shoes or just relax. The chairs also serve as a makeshift nightstand to have a few things close at hand.

We claim our beds by putting our backpacks on them and setting our other belongings such as water bottles, staffs, fanny packs and any recent purchases in close proximity. Since there are no "sets" of bunk beds pushed together in this albergue, my husband chooses the top and I take the bottom. We create our own space and quickly go into our afternoon routine. I take off my sandals and dirty socks and start a "dirty clothes" pile that will contain all the clothes we are now wearing. I discretely remove my money belt and put it in my fanny pack. Not wanting to leave all our possessions unattended, one of us will stay while the other showers.

I usually shower first. I go to my backpack and pull out the Ziploc bags with the soap, washcloth, towel, comb, toothbrush and shampoo. In short - all the things packed when I left the other albergue this morning. The LIFO (Last In, First Out) packing system works well on a trip like this with different stops each day. I also get out the clean set of clothes I will wear the rest of today and tomorrow until we stop.

I locate the bathrooms: four small private rooms with a toilet and a sink and another four rooms with just a shower. Privacy! Wow! I revel in this discovery and claim a shower room which will be mine for the next few minutes. Usually the showers do not have any shelves or places to put the soap and shampoo while washing, so I arrange the necessary items in one of the shower corners before turning on the water. The towel is strategically placed so I can reach it without getting water on my clean clothes. I strip down and take care to set my dirty, dusty clothes away from my clean ones and away from my towel. I reach in and turn on the water and miraculously it becomes warm. There is an actual shower curtain, so I am able to keep the water where it belongs and not get everything else in the room wet. Not all albergues have this luxury, and I have found there is an art to placement of dry clothes while showering. It also helps that I am the first person to shower here today. Those who come later will have to put up with more water spread around and less, if any, warm water.

I luxuriate in the shower, wash my hair and body, dry off and don my clean clothes. I step out of the shower room and go into one of the small toilet rooms to comb my hair and moisturize my face. I do not want to turn into a prune on this journey, so I have made sure I have enough of my facial cleanser and moisturizer to last. My hair will air dry as I go about the rest of my afternoon routine.

Thoroughly refreshed, I return to my bed to find my husband and relate the logistics of showering in this particular albergue. He has been busy looking around and has located the place for washing clothes and for cooking. As he heads off for his shower, I add my dirty clothes to the pile and rummage in my backpack for the laundry soap, sink stopper, and clothes pins. A quick look out the window shows abundant clothes lines set up with a few clothes pins. Since we have our own, I will leave the clothes pins provided for other pilgrims who did not bring their own.

I decide to lie down on the bed for a few minutes while my husband showers. When he returns, we both put on our respective fanny packs with our money belt, camera, cash and credit cards. It may seem we are overdoing it in our diligence to not leave these items unattended, but we felt a bit of caution would save a world of tears if something was stolen. Our valuables were never out of the sight of at least one of us. We were comfortable leaving our backpacks, sleeping bags and clothing, as these items could be replaced if necessary. However, we had no problems. Nothing was ever disturbed. The other pilgrims gave us the same respect we gave to them.

Now both of us are clean and refreshed and there is a pile of dirty clothes to be cleaned. We take the clothes, laundry soap, sink stopper, and clothes pins and head outside to the outdoor "pilas" or clothes washing sinks. These are marvelous sinks which have a ribbed sideboard and are made specifically for hand washing. The water is cold, but is fine for our purposes. There may or may not be a plug provided and pilgrims without one of their own will have to wash their clothes under the running water. I produce our all purpose sink plug and begin to fill the sink. I throw in the bar of laundry soap so it can begin to soften a bit. We each have a set of clothes to be washed and we throw them in the water to soak.

While they are soaking, my husband goes back to retrieve our shoes. We run them under the water to remove the dust and put them in the sun to dry. When the laundry soap has softened, I begin to wash each item by hand. My husband takes the washed item, rinses it under running water and selects a good spot on the clothes line that will receive sun for the rest of the afternoon. Since we arrived early, our clothes will be dry in a couple of hours. On sunny days when we had the time, we would also wash our sleep sheet and pillow case. This kept our sleeping materials fresh and comfortable.

Other pilgrims are beginning to arrive and go through the same processes we have just completed. Bed choice logic is used depending upon the preferences of each individual or group. Soon the albergue is bustling with activity. We have completed our chores and decide to relax a bit. Since it is now approaching 3:00 PM, there is no sense in leaving the albergue. The siesta tradition is practiced throughout Spain and markets, shops and restaurants all close for the hours between about 3:00 and 5:00. The exact times may vary from city to city, store to store, but they do close. Even in the largest cities, everything slows down and stores close during this time.

We each pull out our journal and record our private thoughts and observations for the day. I decide to use the time for its intended purpose and I curl up on my bed for a nap. My husband decides to sit in the sun, so he finds a comfortable spot near the clothes lines to sit and study the guide book and plan tomorrow's journey. Most pilgrims respect the relative quiet in the sleeping rooms, and as other pilgrims come in and see me (and a couple of other people) on the beds relaxing, they limit their talking until they return to the common rooms. I am usually able to sleep for an hour or two.

I awake to a bustle of activity and realize that the person in charge of this albergue has arrived. Word spreads quickly among all who have chosen this as their shelter for the night. I see my husband walking toward me to have me accompany him while we pay and get our credentials stamped. He is still unsure of himself in being able to understand the rapid Spanish, so we go together to make sure there are no misunderstandings. He is the keeper of our credentials, as his fanny pack is larger than mine and they fit much better in his and are not subject to folding or crushing.

We take our credentials, or pilgrim's passport, that we received when we signed up to make the journey back in St. Jean Pied-de-Port, France. It has been stamped every night of the journey by the albergue where we stayed and has become a detailed document of our route. Each albergue has a distinctive stamp design and color. There is a bit of competition among the albergues to have the most interesting representation. The longer one is on the Camino, the more varied and unique the credential becomes.

This particular albergue is run by the local municipality and the person who has just arrived is a volunteer to will spend just a few minutes here gathering money and stamping credentials. The pilgrims form a line and one-by-one present the required fee (about 5 euros for each bed) and the credential. The volunteer looks over each credential and selects an appropriate place for today's stamp. The credentials become a cherished possession for pilgrims and workers in the albergue go out of their way to make sure they look nice. The volunteers look to make sure the stamps are in chronological order and are all facing in the same direction. One can "read" from left to right to see where stops have been made. The volunteer then takes a pen and adds today's date. Now it is official.

As other pilgrims are busy settling in and getting comfortable, we decide to explore the city and find something to eat. The city is starting to come alive again, as all the stores begin to reopen. This is the time we use to shop for any necessities. It is also the time to explore some of the sights the city may offer. There is usually a church or cathedral and we head out to explore it. For this excursion, we are only carrying our fanny packs. All other belongings are safely tucked around our chosen beds in the albergue. It makes walking around much more enjoyable since we do not have to carry the large backpack. We have the rest of the evening to ourselves. Most albergues post a "lights out" time, usually 10:00 or 11:00 PM. My desired bedtime is closer to 9:00, so we will have no problem getting back in time. We spend the next couple of hours exploring whatever the area has to offer. Many times we took the suggestions in our guidebook. Other times, we discovered things not mentioned. Occasionally, the town was small and without attractions. Then we spent the evening relaxing and falling to sleep early.

We chose to find a restaurant for our evening meal on this day, although the albergue did have nice facilities for cooking. We went in search of restaurants with a "pilgrims menu" or "menu del dia" sign in front. In these establishments, we were assured of a nutritious, inexpensive meal, costing about six to nine euros each. One night we splurged and paid eleven euros and had a feast.   The meals usually start with a salad consisting of some combination of lettuce, tomatoes, asparagus, carrots and onions. Olive oil and balsamic vinegar are provided as dressing. The main entrée is a generous portion of chicken, beef or fish, depending on the area and availability, a vegetable and sometimes a potato. Dessert ranges from a piece of fruit to pudding or ice cream.

After a nice meal and some sight seeing and much picture taking, we return to the albergue to bed down for the night. We gather our clothes off the line and find our shoes. We fold and pack our clean items and put away anything else we had taken out of our backpacks. We get the items we will need in the morning and put them within easy reach. We pull out our silk sleep sack and put the pillow case on the pillow. I put my sleeping bag at the foot of my bed for easy reach in case the temperature drops. If it is feeling cool in the albergue already, I spread it out like a blanket and only put it over the top of me rather than trying to crawl into it. I take off my fanny pack and wrap the strap around some part of the headboard or pole supporting the upper bunk. I get into a comfortable position and fall off to sleep quickly, as I am tired from all the day's activity. As I drift off, I make a mental note of the location of a bathroom in case I have to get up during the night to use it.

When lights-out time comes, the whole albergue settles down for the night.   Most pilgrims are tired and soon snores of varying degrees and volumes are heard. I am soon asleep, dreaming of the adventures that I have already experienced and new ones to come.

Experts say it takes 21 days to break a habit or start a new one.   We spent a total of 46 days on this entire walk. After being on the Camino for this amount of time, it seems perfectly natural to sleep in a room with twenty or thirty other people, wake up and walk all day long, and drink water out of a mountain stream.   It no longer seems odd to relieve bodily functions off the side of the trail behind a rock or tree or to talk with perfect strangers along the way. The rising and setting of the sun defined our days and nights. The routine we developed became so natural that returning to our "normal" lives was a task.

Appendix B

Spiritual Side Trips

Spiritual Side Trips

What is intensely spiritual to one person can be mundane to the next. And conversely, what is totally ordinary to one can be incredibly inspiring to another. There are thousands of possibilities for spiritual side trips, both physical and virtual. While traveling the Camino both my husband and I experienced things we found inspiring and spiritual. Every pilgrim's journey will be unique. There is no way to give a comprehensive guide to the spiritual part of the journey. Everyone should follow their heart, and if something beckons, explore it.

There were many things beckoning to us and we followed. However, three experiences stand out every time I reflect on the journey and I would like to relate them here and how they affected me.

The first happened early, on our fifth day out of Saint Jean Pied-de-Port. We had just left the small town of Uterga and were headed to Puenta la Reina. In Pamplona we had met a volunteer from the US who was working at the albergue. He told us about an interesting twelfth century church that was only a few kilometers off the regular Camino. We decided to go and it was well worth the trouble. It is the Hermitage of Our Lady of Eunate (Ermita de Nuestra Señora de Eunate) and it was easy to follow the signs, as many pilgrims make this side trip.

On the morning we arrived, the church was packed with two busloads of tourists who had just arrived. The crowd of people was a bit overwhelming after walking through almost deserted countryside for several hours. However, this turned out to be a blessing, because we were able to overhear the guide's talk about the history of the church. This information was not available in our guidebook or at the church itself. No one knows for sure who built the church. It is built in a Romanesque style which was popular around the twelfth century. It is built in an octagon shape with a small central building, surrounded by two outer "walls" also in the octagon shape. The outer wall has one entrance. The inner wall has four places with an archway to go from the outer to the inner passageway. The entrance to the inner building is on the opposite side of the entrance to the outer wall. We heard the guide tell the tourists about the local legends concerning the building. To enter the inner building, people would remove their shoes when entering the outer wall and walk three times counterclockwise in the outer passageway around the building. We decided to follow the legendary ritual to enter the building. This area was lush with grass, so this was a pleasant experience. Then, the legend says that you must go into the next passageway and walk three times clockwise. This ground in the inner area was covered with small cobblestones. In bare feet, it was not comfortable and took longer to circumvent. Finally, the inner building is entered.

The diameter of the inside of the church was only about 25 feet. It is sparsely furnished with a simple altar and six or eight benches with no backs. The ceiling is high with small slits for light to enter. Consequently, it is cool inside compared to the outside temperature. We had waited until the busloads of people left before performing the entrance ritual, so when we entered, we were the only people in the church. We both found the place to be calming and conducive to relaxing and meditating. We spent a few minutes just soaking in the calming effect and looking around the room. We were reluctant to leave, but we had more miles to walk that day.

There is an additional building near the church where the modern day caretakers live. On a small table outside this building, pilgrims can put the stamp for Eunate in their Pilgrim's Passport. On the day we visited it was interesting and relaxing, but I did not think it especially inspiring at the time. It is only upon returning home and talking about my experiences with friends that I realized its impact. It is one of the first things that comes to mind when friends ask me about the journey. I can still go back there in my mind and re-experience it. That may be the real indication that the place had an effect on me.

***

The village of Rabanal del Camino hosts a small monastery of Benedictine monks. Three monks, to be exact. On some days they have a special ceremony comprised of Gregorian chants. We were lucky enough to be there on a day when one of these ceremonies was being celebrated. Word spread among the pilgrims who were staying in the town that the ceremony would begin at 7:00 PM. The church building dated back several centuries and had limited seating capacity, so we made it a point to arrive a little early. One of the monks was talking with the pilgrims who were milling around, waiting for the ceremony to begin. He was multilingual and spoke to the pilgrims in German, French, Spanish and English. As he located a pilgrim with a different language, he asked them if they would participate in the ceremony by reading a passage in their native tongue. Everyone asked, agreed, and the ceremony became an international event. Each pilgrim in turn read a passage, which was followed by chanting by the monks. The voices of the three monks filled the monastery and captivated all who were present. The time went by quickly and we were reluctant to leave the charming atmosphere. However, other experiences were awaiting and so we left the church and went to bed with the melodic chanting still ringing in our heads.

***

Another memorable experience happened twenty days later in the beautiful city of León. We stayed at the main albergue, in the Convento de las Carbajalas. This convent is run by Benedictine nuns who have strict rules regarding how the albergue is run, but this also offers one advantage. It was the lovely benefit of having the opportunity to go to a Pilgrim's blessing given by the nuns themselves. We were told to be back in the convent by 9:30PM sharp, as they would close the doors, and anyone not inside would not be let in. We came back on time and chose to attend the blessing with about 25 other people. A man (probably a monk or padre) rounded us up and took us over to the chapel where the nuns were waiting. One nun came out to explain to us what the ceremony would be like. Not being Catholic, I was ready for anything. They proceeded to hand out little booklets with the ceremony printed inside in different languages. They had Spanish (of course), French and German. When I asked for "¿Inglès?" the quick reply was "¡NO, Español!" and a Spanish version was thrust in my hand. All the English speaking pilgrims learned more Spanish that night.

The ceremony was inspring. There were about 12 nuns whose average age had to be in the 70s. They sang for us and the music reverberated and rebounded in the gothic ceiling creating a harmony of harmonies that was enchanting. They then said some prayers and gave us a little talk about the meaning of the Camino and how we are on sacred ground. It was magical. It was, of course, all in Spanish and as I understood most of it, I could give a couple of other English speakers a quick translation. After these prayers we returned to the convent to bed down for the night. We were truly blessed. The music and the sound of their voices still reverberates in my mind and takes me back to that special evening.

***

One of the most inspiring things for me took place almost every day of the journey. As we started our trek every morning, there would invariable be wildflowers along the trail. More often than not, red poppies would be included in the bouquet of the day. At times there were fields of poppies, at other times they lined the path, seeming to cheer us on with their bright, friendly blossoms. Poppies have come to be a symbol of the Camino for me, along with the traditional cockle shell and staff. The poppies seemed to exude energy and any time I was tired or having problems with an uphill climb, a poppy along the path would make me smile and I would have the energy for anything.

My spiritual memories will be different from yours. The best way to experience something spiritually is to be open to the unexpected. When things do not happen as planned, sometimes the alternatives turns out to be better. I know I do not always know what is best for me. I would rather have infinite possibilities, and allow things I may not have considered to come into manifestation. Be open and enjoy what comes your way.

Appendix C

Cost of the Trip

Cost of the Trip

The cost of the trip will be unique for each person depending on many factors. For this reason, I have constructed a few worksheets that can be used to determine your approximate costs. These sheets are based on the information and advice given in this book. For a printable copy, go to my webpage at www.CheriPowell.com. I hope you find them useful

Money you will spend to get yourself to Spain:

Transportation and Insurance	Number of People	Cost per person	Total
Travel insurance policy			
Plane ticket to Spain			
Transport to starting point - bus			
Transport to starting point - train			
Taxi to hotel	-----------		
Total			

Money you will spend getting started and along the Camino on a daily basis:

Daily Expenses	Estimated cost each (in Euros)	Number of days	Amount per day	Total
Food - prepared at albergues	3 to 5			
Food - Pilgrim's Menu	5 to 11			
Arrival nights in hotel before traveling Camino	75 to 100			

Departure nights in hotel after traveling Camino	75 to 100		
Estimated nights to stay in Church-run albergues	0 to 5		
Estimated nights to stay in municipal albergues	3 to 7		
Estimated nights to stay in private albergues	5 to 11		
Estimated nights to stay in hotels along the Camino	20 to 50		
Estimated incidentals (replenish shampoo, etc.)			
Total			

This can be used as a shopping guide for items you might need to purchase for the trip. Each person should use one copy of this list. Space has been provided to add any items that are not already mentioned.

	Already Have	Need to Buy	Amount Spent
You will need:			
Footwear			
Backpack			
Something for sleeping			
Fanny pack			
Money belt			
Clothes			
2 pair of shorts			
2 tops to wear with the shorts			
2 bras (for women)			

2 pair underpants			
1 pair long pants with zip off legs			
1 long sleeve pullover running top			
1 long sleeve shirt			
2 pair of socks			
Toiletries and grooming products			
Body soap			
Shampoo			
Deodorant			
Comb and/or brush			
Toothbrush			
Toothpaste/tooth soap			
Dental floss			
Nail brush			
Emery board			
Bug repellant (general purpose)			
Bug repellant (bedbugs)			
Sunscreen			
Facial cleanser (for women)			
Facial moisturizer (for women)			
Shaving kit (complete kit for men, razor for women)			
Tissues/Toilet Paper			
Body lotion			
Towel and washcloth			
Guidebook			
Sunglasses			
Medicines – prescriptions			
Medicines – OTC			
Extra prescription glasses			
Miscellaneous items			

	Already Have	Need to Buy	Amount Spent
Clothes pins			
Clothes line			
Safety pins			
Swiss Army knife			
Lip balm			
Throat lozenges			
Soap for washing clothes			
Flat sink plug			
You might want:			
Camera			
Batteries			
Extra clothes			
Rain poncho			
Makeup			
Something from home			
Spanish phrase book			
Personal journal			
First aid kit			
Band aids			
Moleskin for blisters			
Antiseptic cream			
Elastic bandage			
Flashlight			
Ear plugs			
Neck cooler			
Hat			
Sleep mask			
Watch			
Air mattress/sleep pad			
GPS unit			
Personal Energy Generator			

Cell Phone			
Extras that make a difference:			
Zip lock bags			
Space-saver bags			
Duct tape			
Handiwipes			
Total			

I hope this list has been helpful and you have a joyous journey.

Appendix D

Further Reading and Internet Links

Further Reading and Internet Links

Books

Coelho, Paulo. <u>The Pilgrimage</u>. San Francisco: Harper Collins, 1995.

Coffey, Thomas F., LInda Kay Davidson, and Maryjane Dunn. The Miracles of Saint James. New York: Italiza Press, 1996.

MacLaine, Shirley. <u>The Camino, A Journey of the Spirit</u>. New York: Pocket Books, 2000.

Melczer, William. <u>The Pilgrim's Guide to Santiago de Compostela</u>. 1993. New York: Italica Press, 1993.

Metzger, Bruce M., and Michael D. Coogan. <u>The Oxford Companion to the Bible</u>. New York: Oxford University Press, 1993.

Miller, Madelieine S., and J. Lane Miller. <u>Harper's Bible Dictionary</u>. Sixth. New York: Harper & Brothers, 1959.

Mullins, Edwin. <u>The Pilgrimage to Santiago</u>. New York: Interlink Books, 2001.

Nardo, Don. <u>Life on a Medieval Pilgrimage,</u> San Diego: Lucent Books. 1996

Thurston, S.J., Herbert. "Saint James the Greater."<u>Butler's lives of the Saints</u>. Volume III. 1980.

Vinayo Gonzalez, Antonio. <u>Camino de Santiago, Guia del peregrino a pie, a caballo, en bicicleta y en coche</u>. Leon, Espana: Edilesa, 1999.

Interrnet Links

Author web page

Visit for chapter illustrations and downloadable spreadsheets
www.CheriPowell.com

Camino Groups

These sites are groups that can be joined to get specific questions answered.
http://groups.yahoo.com/group/Santiagobis/
http://groups.yahoo.com/group/Ultreya/
http://www.mundicamino.com/ingles/
http://www.caminodesantiago.me/board/

Camino sites

http://santiago-compostela.net/

Culture Shock

Some sites to further exlplain sysmptoms and what to do about them.
http://www.herneconsultants.com/cultureshock.htm
http://www.uwec.edu/Counsel/pubs/shock.htm
http://danger.mongabay.com/culture_shock.htm

Jet Lag

These sites explain the symptoms and tell how to avoid them.
http://www.nojetlag.com/jetlag3.html
http://www.bodyclock.com/
http://gorp.away.com/gorp/travel/skills/jet_lag.htm

Maps

View all routes to Santiago
http://www.backpack45.com/images/mappassport.jpg
An excellent source for route and elevation maps.
http://www.elcaminosantiago.com/Camino-Santiago-Maps.htm
Map showing French Route
http://www.backpack45.com/images/caminomap.jpg

Saint James

A few sites that offer information on Saint James.
http://news.bbc.co.uk/2/hi/europe/3680331.stm
http://www.csj.org.uk/apostle.htm
http://www.saint-jacques.info/anglais/spotlights.htm

Spanish customs and norms

http://gospain.about.com/od/spanishlife/tp/spanish_customs_traditio
ns_spain.htm
http://www.idealspain.com/pages/information/culture.htm
http://www.mapsofworld.com/spain/traditions-in-spain.html
http://www.marbellaguide.com/spanish-traditions-an-overview.html

Spanish postal codes
http://www.csj.org.uk/faqs.htm#intouch

State Department

These sites give information about all countries in the world and issue travel warnings when there are problems in an area.

http://www.state.gov/r/pa/ei/bgn/ - Scroll down and click on "Spain." This will give some brief background and history about the country

Travel web sites to get your plane ticket or your hotel

http://www.orbitz.com/
http://www.skyauction.com/
http://www.priceline.com/
http://www.travelocity.com/
http://www.planetickets.com/

Notes

Visit for chapter illustrations and downloadable spreadsheets
<u>www.CheriPowell.com</u>

Notes
Visit for chapter illustrations and downloadable spreadsheets
<u>www.CheriPowell.com</u>

Notes
Visit for chapter illustrations and downloadable spreadsheets
www.CheriPowell.com

Notes

Visit for chapter illustrations and downloadable spreadsheets
www.CheriPowell.com

Notes

Visit for chapter illustrations and downloadable spreadsheets
www.CheriPowell.com

17839717R00096

Made in the USA
Lexington, KY
30 September 2012